Scenario planning in a week

Scenario planning in a week

Michiel de Vries & Jeroen Toet

Jester Foresight

CONTENTS

1 |

Foreword

“ Wondering about your organization's future? What keeps ”
you up at night?

When I talk with decision-makers, this simple question often gets them talking about how uncertain the future is and how hard it is for their leadership teams to agree on what to do. It is a big challenge that makes them feel stuck and concerned.

For almost a decade, and through multiple roles, I have worked closely with Michiel, Jeroen, and the team at Jester Strategy. I have seen how powerful scenario planning can be in making sense of the future and helping teams arrive at future-proof strategic choices.

This book is all about making scenario planning practical and useful. It helps leadership teams deal with uncertainty and make decisive, yet flexible plans. Over the years, I have met numerous people who previously used some version of scenario planning. Too often people were somewhat disappointed, because they struggled to utilize the insights in a meaningful way. That is a missed opportunity. This book addresses that, making scenario planning accessible and applicable. Through clear steps, examples, and templates it shows how to turn scenarios into tangible plans. That is where things really come together!

I have applied this book's methodology in numerous projects in Australia with leadership teams from a wide variety of sectors, from resources to agriculture and from regulators to universities. They have told me this approach helped them in five main ways:

1. **Seeing the Future Together**: Leadership teams often struggle to agree on what the future will be like. But when they work together to address uncertainties and imagine different futures, it helps them create a better and shared understanding.
2. **Planning for Change**: The world is changing in ways we cannot accurately predict. Scenario planning helps leaders make plans that work no matter what happens.
3. **Faster Planning**: Planning can take a long time, but scenario planning speeds things up. By thinking about different futures, teams can converge on assumptions and choices faster and are able to adjust in a timely manner.
4. **Everyone Owns the Plan**: When there is a shared understanding of the future and how to navigate it, the plan becomes everyone's. This makes it stronger and more exciting.
5. **Thinking Outside the Box**: Successful organizations recognize changes and adapt quickly. Scenario planning helps them practice this by thinking about different futures. It is like rehearsing for change.

I have learned a lot from the Dutch version of this book and so I am excited that it is now accessible to more people around the world. I have no doubt you will find this guide helpful for you and your organization as you deal with a changing and uncertain future. I heartily recommend this book.

Sander van Amelsvoort - Partner Jester Strategy

Preface

It had to happen one day, us writing a book about scenario planning. We have so much to tell about this insightful and powerful method to explore the future with. Since the start of our consultancy careers, we have both used scenario planning for numerous applications. Whether it is for inspiring radical innovation, formulating long term strategy, testing investment decisions, career choices, or just being able to better anticipate the future, scenario planning is the ultimate method to enable you to prepare for an unpredictable future and make future-proof decisions.

Until now we never really considered publishing a book about our approach and experience. For a solid reason. There already are numerous books about scenario planning. However, as informative and thorough as these are, we encountered few books that offered clear, concise, and practical advise to put scenario planning into practice. We believe that learning by doing always works best. Therefore, we have written a book that will guide you along a scenario planning process step by step. One that also offers you the tools, templates, and tips and tricks from our decades of experience so you are well-equipped to start your own scenario project.

This book follows the approach that we at Jester Strategy have honed and put into practice in hundreds of projects over the years. Our approach works for any kind of organization, for Fortune 500 companies, local governments, or NGOs alike. We are confident our approach will surely work for you as well. Whether you want to innovate, stress-test your strategy, monitor your external environment, or simply want to have a strategic conversation regarding the future with your colleagues or stakeholders, this book will not disappoint.

We had a great time writing this book. But truth be told, we could never have done it without all those organizations whose scenario projects we were fortunate enough to have supported, all our colleagues with whom we often exchange ideas at our office's lunch table, and the many authors who have previously published about working with scenarios. To all of these, we are immensely grateful.

We hope you enjoy reading this book and that it inspires you to develop and apply scenarios yourself. We are curious what you think of this book and invite you to share your thoughts and experiences with us. If you need any help or if you have any questions please feel free to reach out to us.

Michiel de Vries – *m.vries@jesterstrategy.com*
Jeroen Toet- *j.toet@jesterstrategy.com*

Amersfoort, The Netherlands, September 2023

Introduction to scenario planning

This book is about developing and applying external scenarios. This process is also known as *scenario planning*. However, many different definitions and conceptions of scenarios exist. When we use the word scenarios, we mean imaginative narratives of the future. Because the future is uncertain and cannot be precisely predicted, you always need to explore and consider multiple possible futures.

In this book we will present an approach to develop scenarios you can use in decision making, in developing strategy, for innovation, or to simply underpin a dialogue regarding the future with your management team and/or stakeholders.

What are scenarios?

We certainly are not the first who have written about scenario planning. Harvard professor Michael Porter describes scenarios as an internally consistent view of what the future might turn out to be [Porter, 1985]. Peter Schwartz, one of Shell's scenario planning pioneers, describes it as a disciplined method for imaging possible futures in which the decisions of an organization may be played out. He regards it as a powerful tool for structuring perceptions of alternative future environments that need to be incorporated in decision making [Schwartz, 1991]. A central theme in all these definitions is that a scenario is neither a choice nor a prediction. Scenarios are conceivable futures that arise from the most important uncertainties an organization is confronted with in its external environment. Above all, the best scenarios are developed collaboratively so team members can learn from one another's expectations of the future.

SCENARIOS ARE	SCENARIOS ARE NOT
✓ **External** realities that **cannot** be influenced	X **Choices** for certain directions
✓ **Explorations** of the future (with uncertainty at its basis)	X **Predictions** of the future
	X **Visions** or strategic plans
✓ **Extreme** yet plausible futures	

Table 1: What are scenarios?

Why use scenarios?

You might think by now, so how can scenarios help me when they are neither choices nor solutions? Well, in fact, scenarios can lay a great foundation to arrive at future-proof choices or solutions. They can assist you in exploring the future and, in doing so, identify multiple arenas in which the future might play out. Good scenarios will stimulate you to think about opportunities, threats, risks, and strategic options. Furthermore, they can provide a frame of reference for decision making, as ideas or strategic options that have a good fit with multiple scenarios can be deemed futureproof. Such ideas are robust, as they will be relevant in multiple plausible futures.

Scenarios capture uncertainty

Scenarios are always based on trends and uncertainties in the external environment, the world of developments and changes that can hardly be influenced by a single organization, let alone individual people. The impact of such external developments on the success of companies has significantly grown since the turn of the century. American research illustrates, for instance, that half of the returns of big industrial corporations can be attributed to external influences, such as economic and political shifts or changes in the competitive environment. A few recent examples can readily illustrate the impact of uncertainties, such as the 2008 financial crisis, Brexit, the covid-19 pandemic, the war in Ukraine, or the current period (2023) of scarcities and high inflation. The issue is not whether organizations will be affected by these external developments. Rather, it is how they will deal with them.

Using scenarios in five simple steps

Scenarios offer organizations a tool to manage, even profit from, uncertainty. We have tons to say on this, but we rather want to encourage you to experience the benefits of scenario planning yourself. In developing and applying scenarios we always follow a set methodology. This systematic approach can be applied to various issues and themes. Within this approach there is plenty of room for the ever so important creativity and imagination. The best scenarios are always developed at the intersection where rational analyses and creative imagination meet.

The five steps of developing and applying scenarios are the following:

1. Define scope
2. Explore the environment
3. Determine key uncertainties
4. Develop scenarios
5. Apply scenarios

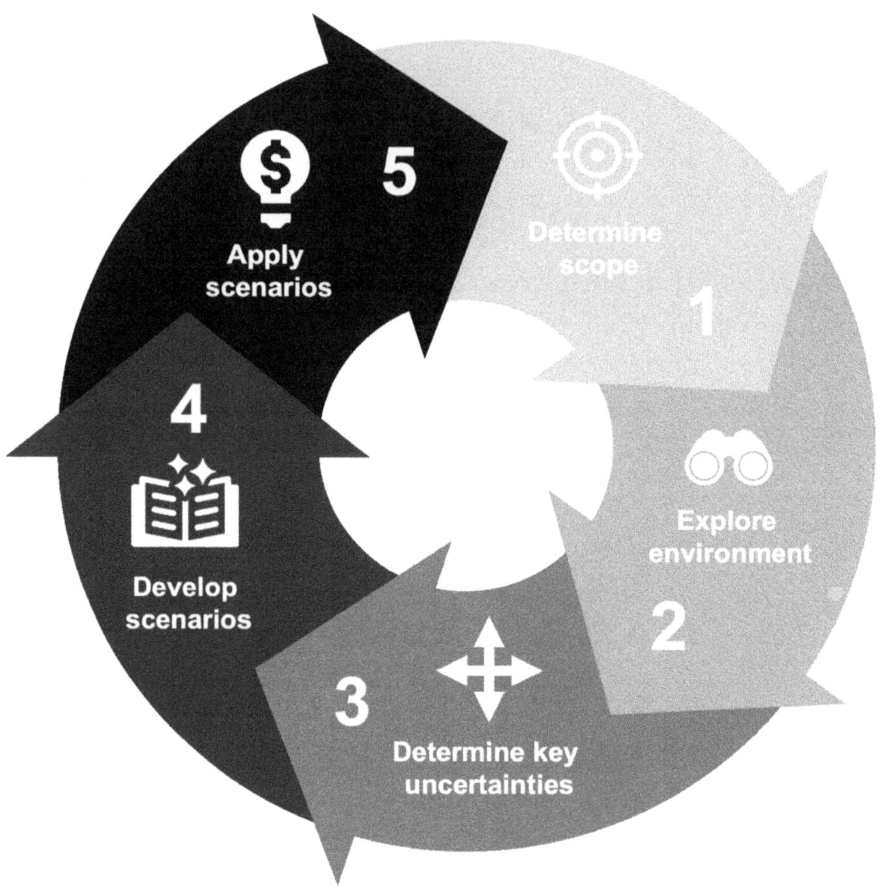

Figure 1: the five steps of scenario planning

1. Determine the scope

A clear scope is of the utmost importance when developing scenarios. A scope provides the necessary focus. During the scoping phase you will consider what will be the focal question you would like the scenarios to provide you an answer to. A focal question is a fundamental question about the future. For example, what will be the impact of new technologies on our business model? Or what will society look like? The scope will also determine how far into the future you would like to peer, which actors can exert influence on the focal questions and therefore need to be studied, and which boundaries will apply. A good scope will detail what the scenarios should include but also exclude. The scope will be an anchor point, a frame of reference, for the subsequent steps of the scenario planning process. One that you will return to regularly.

2. Explore the environment

Once you have a set clear scope, you can start exploring the external environment. You will look for relevant developments that cannot be influenced by your organization. Scenario planning is all about thinking *outside-in*. The external environment consists of multiple layers. The outer layer is the macro environment; often consisting of political, economic, social, technological, ecological, and demographic developments. A bit closer to home for organizations is the direct environment. This layer can entail changes in terms of consumer preferences, supplier dynamics, or the rise of new competitors or substitutes. Stakeholders of your organization are also part of the external enviroment. If their behavior is unpredictable, has an impact, and cannot be influenced, then it is advised to include their behavior in the analysis.

3. Determine key uncertainties

In many cases, exploring the external environment will result in an extensive list of developments. Therefore, it is important to reduce this to a set of key uncertainties. These are developments that will not only have a large impact on the focal question of the scope but also display a large degree of uncertainty. Ideally, key uncertainties also will influence a large number of other developments you identified. Key uncertainties are major game changers. They are highly uncertain factors that can cause an entire system to shift. Some common key uncertainties are the degree of (de)globalization, economic development, the adoption (rate) of a certain technology, or the degree of solidarity within a society.

One, two, or three key uncertainties can form the basis of a set of scenarios. When one key uncertainty forms the foundation of scenarios, you will need to develop two scenarios, based on the two extreme ends of one axis. These 'what if' scenarios are particularly relevant when an organization is confronted with one dominant uncertainty. When two key uncertainties are relevant, you will need to develop a 2x2 matrix, consisting of four quadrants that will form the framework for your scenarios (see figure 2).

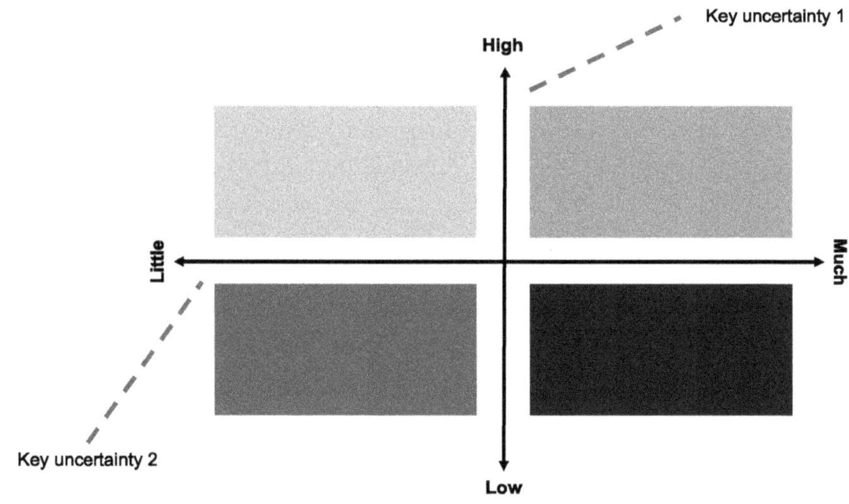

Figure 2: a 2x2 matrix based on two key uncertainties

We are a proponent of working with four scenarios. Four scenarios enable you to explore four different corners of the future playing field, so to speak. The high degree of uncertainty most companies are faced with nowadays requires looking at multiple futures. Working with three key uncertainties, and therefore eight (2^3) scenarios, is also possible. However, in our experience, the added complexity does not outweigh the benefits of possible additional insights they might provide. Considering four scenarios is often rich and challenging enough for most strategists!

4. Develop scenarios

Once you have selected a scenario framework, you will develop and detail the scenarios. This often is an inspirational step, as both logic and imagination will come into play. It is not easy to develop plausible and inspiring narratives for four completely different scenarios. A good scenario consists of three elements. First you need a chronology (a 'road to'). What events could make this scenario a reality? Describing the characteristics of the scenario is the next step. What does the world look like? What will consumers want? What position will certain stakeholders assume? Finally, you will formulate some crucial challenges, meant to trigger and inspire readers to think about relevant strategic responses.

A scenario is a narrative of a series of possible events and characteristics but does not necessarily consist of mere text alone. The best scenarios often are accompanied by visualizations, such as headlines, infographics, 'a day in the life' of a customer or citizen, or even a video. The more a scenario user can relate to the scenarios, the better her or his strategic ideas will be.

5. Apply scenarios

In the fifth step of our approach, the scenarios will be used for their intended purpose. If the objective is to use the scenarios in order to learn and innovate, then the scenarios will be used to inspire and generate new ideas. If the goal is stress-testing strategy, then the organization's choices will be tested against the scenarios to see whether these choices are relevant or beneficial in each scenario. If so, they can be deemed robust/futureproof. Is the purpose risk management, then one will explore which risks for successfully implementing the strategy can arise in the various scenarios.

Standing on the shoulders of giants

This book will be focused on learning by doing and certainly does not aspire to describe an extensive history of the methodology. Yet, just like Isaac Newton, we cannot deny that we have stood on the shoulders of giants in crafting our approach to scenarios. This approach is highly influenced by what we have learned from organizations that have developed scenario planning and turned it into the powerful tool for strategy it is today.

The foundation was laid by the RAND Corporation, which used scenarios in relation to Cold War military strategies. The Club of Rome also used scenario planning in their famous 'Limits to Growth' study. However, it was Shell that refined the methodology in the 1970s and 1980s and actually introduced it to boardrooms. Many consultancy firms have subsequently refined it. We have learned the most from Global Business Network (GBN).

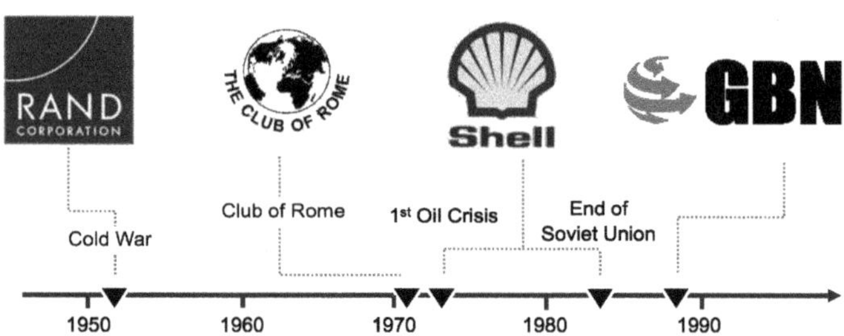

Figure 3: organizations that have developed and refined scenario planning

The reason why scenarios are such a helpful strategic tool is that they can serve to inspire as well as to (stress)test. Often, the most challenging and extreme scenarios will inspire the beste ideas and strategic options. The scenarios can subsequently assist in formulating a robust strategy. A robust, or futureproof, strategy is a mix of choices that adequately prepares the organization for all scenarios. Of course, taking risks is the essence of entrepreneurship but scenarios will help in taking these more deliberately.

How should I read this book?

This book will start with a few real-life examples, both from our personal lives as well as our company. The examples in chapter 4 will hopefully make clear that you can use scenario planning for a wide variety of subjects and purposes.

Chapters 5 to 10 will form the core of the book. In these chapters we will explain how you can develop and apply a set of useful and inspiring scenarios. Chapter 5 will go into what you need in terms of preparation. The remaining chapters will detail the five steps of scenario planning. We have tried to structure the chapters for easy practical use. We always start with a bit of background, after which we will outline the approach, provide some easy-to-use workshop formats, and share a few 'golden rules'.

Scenarios are not only a means to arrive at futureproof choices but are also a helpful instrument to monitor change in the external environment. Chapter 11, therefore, will explain how you can use scenarios for an 'early warning system' to quickly and timely identify and adapt to change.

We hope this book will inspire you to develop scenarios yourself. In doing so, we urge you to follow the approach closely. The methodology is layered and often nuanced and is comprised of certain analyses you should not skip. To assist you as much as possible, we have developed a list of key phrases that we will use in this book (see figure 4). If at any point you lose track of things, you can always relate back to this figure to get you back on track.

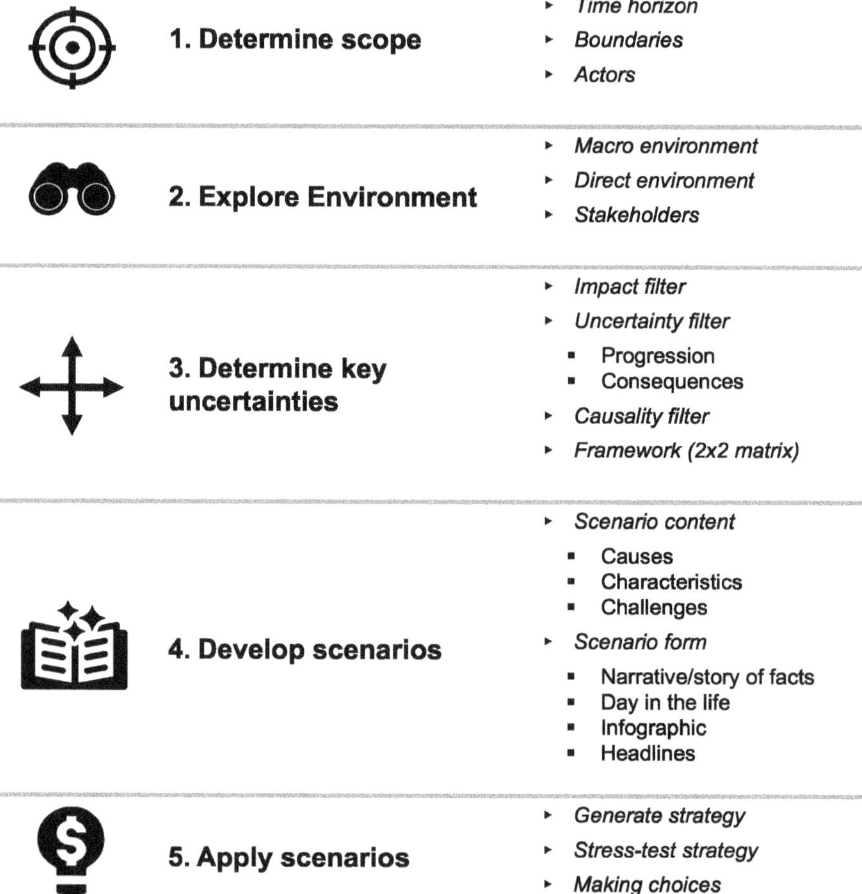

Figure 4: key phrases per step

4 |

Scenarios in practice

Scenarios assist individuals and organizations in preparing for change and uncertainty. By means of anticipating multiple possible future environments, one can make choices more deliberately and judiciously. Sometimes those choices can be 'no regret' choices that are relevant and beneficial in every scenario. Sometimes those choices can be rather risky; choices that position you extremely well for one or two scenarios, but can be quite ill-considered for the others. In such a case, scenarios will at least assist you in considering and mitigating these risks. For instance, through using the scenarios to develop a 'plan B'. You can use scenario planning in different situations and for different purposes. In this chapter we will provide you with examples from our personal and professional lives.

Scenarios and career planning

After Michiel graduated at the beginning of this millennium, he got a job at a large consultancy firm. Being a junior, he was handed a wide variety of tasks. One day he would be making slide decks for presentations, the next day he would do desk research or contribute to developing new consultancy services. After a few years, he realized that he was happiest when he could share knowledge, in all kinds of ways. He still had not fully formed a clear picture of what he wanted his career to look like, of the profession he ultimately would like to be in. Michiel wanted to ensure that he would be making smart choices, spending time on and attention to people, subjects, services, and skills that would be of benefit throughout his career.

He decided to develop a set of scenarios for his career. There were numerous factors that were highly uncertain and were largely determined by opportunities and circumstances in his environment. Should he stay in the Netherlands or work abroad? Should he specialize in a certain industry or competence? Should he continue to be a consultant? The two most uncertain factors for his career at that time were 1. whether he would remain an employee or become an entrepreneur and 2. whether he would focus on education and training or on advising companies.

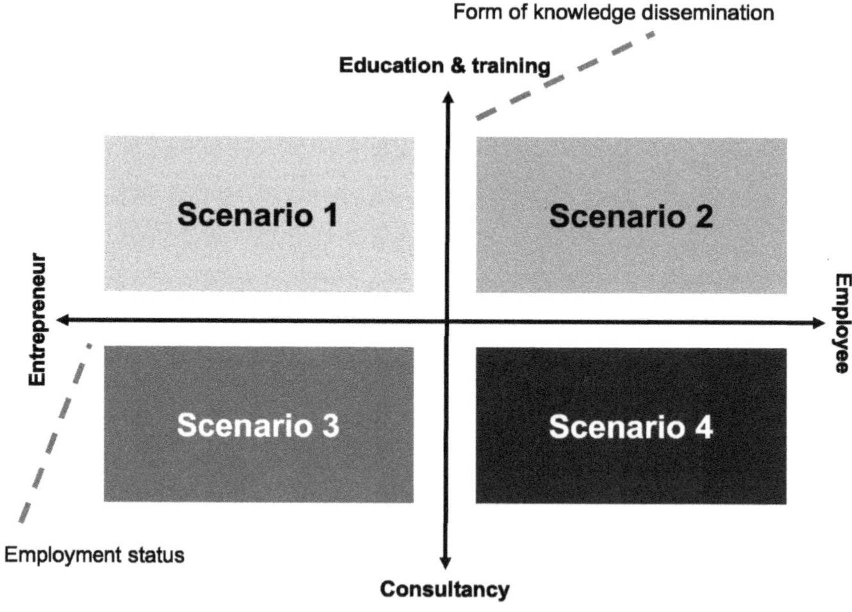

Figure 5: scenarios for Michiel's career

He incorporated these two uncertainties into a scenario framework, resulting in four scenarios for his career. He could focus on education and training. In combination with entrepreneurship that could, for instance, mean that he could be a trainer or share holder in a training and coaching firm. Combined with being an employee, this could mean he should be a teacher or professor. Alternatively, he could focus on giving advise. He could do this in the guise of owner of a consultancy firm or as an employee of a consultancy firm.

Michiel was twenty-four when he made these scenarios. He was determined to make future-proof choices; choices that are relevant in every scenario. And he succeeded. For instance, he decided to only take on projects in which he would have direct contact with the client. That way, he could build the network he needed, preparing himself for the two entrepreneurial scenarios. He also decided to spend much time on publications and on training facilitation. He wanted to get a feel for the world of education and retain the option of specializing as a trainer or teacher. All of this also meant he sometimes had to say no to certain projects. He would decline projects that would not offer him new knowledge and expertise, relations, or opportunities for publication.

Scenarios and big investments

When Michiel started his own firm, Jester Strategy, he suddenly had to think about mobility. When he left his old firm, he had to hand in the keys of the company car. Now he had to look for a new car himself. He started to list some requirements, some pros and cons. Some things he knew for certain. For instance, he would use the car for four years. In those four years he would assume a depreciation to 40% of the list price. He also wanted a diesel-powered car. What kind and make of car, however, he was still unsure of. There were some important variables he first had to consider before buying one. The first variable was the annual mileage. Would he have to drive a lot, or would it be minimal? The second variable was the fuel price. His 'base case' assumptions were an annual mileage of 20,000 kilometers and a diesel price of € 1.30 per liter. After some extensive catalogue browsing, he landed on two cars he considered.

- An SUV with a list price of € 50,000 and a fuel consumption of 15 liter/100 km

- A station wagon with a list price of € 65,000 and a fuel consumption of 8 liter/100 km

Michiel decided to calculate the business case for both cars and started crunching some numbers. With a diesel price of € 1.30 per liter and with an annual mileage of 20,000 km, the SUV would be the clear winner; saving him € 3,000 when compared to the station wagon. As the brand's importer was a client of his, he left to their HQ to order it directly with them.

While on his way, doubt set in. He realized he did not take uncertainties adequately into account when making the initial business case. What if fuel prices would skyrocket? Or plummet? And what if he would drive considerably more than 20,000 km per year? Or, conversely, a lot less? He decided to turn home and start going over some scenarios. He decided to draft up a scenario framework based on his most important uncertainties. On one of the axes would be the fuel price. A high fuel price Michiel defined as € 2.50 per liter; a low one as € 1.20. The other axis would deal with his annual mileage. Based on data from previous years, he expected a low mileage to be 20,000 km; a high one would amount to 60,000 km.

Michiel had to make some new calculations. He made business cases for both cars in all four possible scenarios. Soon it dawned on him that in three out of four scenarios the station wagon actually came out on top. Only in a scenario of low fuel costs and low mileage would the SUV be the better choice. As all scenarios could easily become reality in the next four years, he decided to assign a 25% probability to all four of them. If he multiplied the outcomes of each scenario with that 25% chance and added up all the outcomes, then the station wagon would definitely be the most futureproof choice. Looking back on it now - a decade later, it surely was.

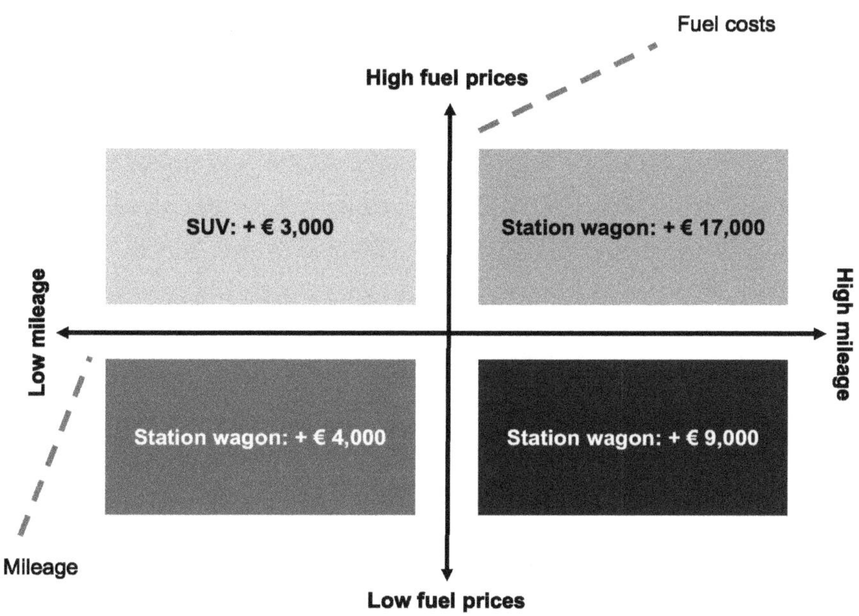

Figure 6: investment decision (car costs) scenarios

Scenarios and strategic positioning

In 2013, Jeroen joined Michiel's firm as one of the first employees. Being a scenario planner at heart, he wanted not only to develop future scenarios for clients but for the firm itself as well. The company needed a solid frame of reference to make the right choices regarding strategic positioning towards the future. To which industries should Jester Strategy cater? What kinds of clients would be targeted? What products and services should the firm offer?

With their colleagues, Jeroen and Michiel started identifying the most relevant external developments. All sorts of developments were explored. Ranging from political developments to new competitors and shifting client preferences. Each development was carefully considered. What would the impact be on the young firm? Which developments were certain, which ones were uncertain? Additionally, how were the developments interrelated? In the end, two key uncertainties, were identified. After a rebound after the 2008 financial crisis, the Dutch economy took another hit and was still in a downward spiral in 2013. Would this prove to be a short-lived economic downturn or was the country in structural economic stagnation? The future of strategy consulting was another topic of debate. Would it still be seen as a craft in which professional experience and expertise and human interaction would be front and center? Or would technologies, such as algorithms, make the 'traditional' consultant obsolete?

Jeroen drew up the 2x2 scenario framework and used our tried-and-true method to develop four scenarios. For each scenario Jeroen and Michiel identified the opportunities, threats, and challenges for their firm. Once they had a clear picture of those, they started formulating strategic options. They explicitly chose to be prepared for each (and therefore all) possible scenario. They simply could not afford to put all their eggs in just one basket, so to speak.

Scenario planning did not fail them. For instance, Michiel and Jeroen chose to serve both private and public sectors. This would make the firm less dependent on economic cycles. They also chose to proactively invest in technology. In addition to their consulting practice, they developed online tools that they could leverage in a situation in which there would be less demand for consultants of flesh and blood. Little did they know then that a global pandemic would drive up demand for such online tools nearly a decade later. All in all, scenarios have helped their firm to position itself robustly.

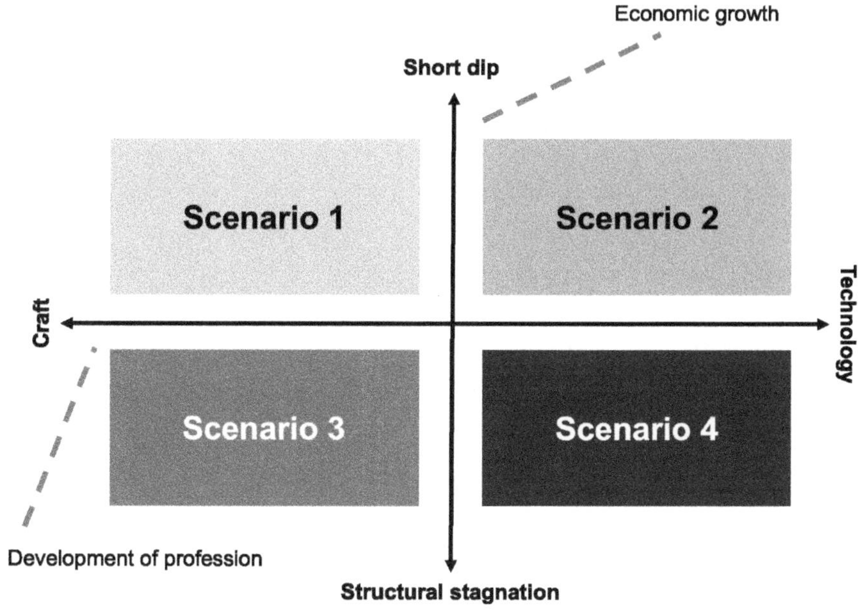

Figure 7: Scenarios for our firm

Scenarios for Sunergie

Throughout the years, we have applied scenario planning so many times that offering this approach to our clients was a no-brainer. One of our clients that could not wait to apply scenario planning was an importer of solar panels and home batteries. In this book we will call them Sunergie. We will frequently use Sunergie's case to illustrate key steps of the method.

When we were contracted by Sunergie, that company was recently passed along from its founder Fred to his children, Martin and Lisa. Sunergie has grown significantly after it was founded by Fred but the last few years the revenues have plateaued. Even more worrisome, the margins have eroded. Therefore, when they took over, Martin and Lisa were faced with some fundamental questions. How could they grow and (re)develop the company? What products should it carry? Should they remain an independent importer or should they integrate more into the value chain? How could they reduce the (over)reliance on certain markets and products? Should they perhaps produce products themselves? All their questions could be boiled down to one leading strategic question, how can we retain our position as a leading importer during the energy transition?

Together with their management team we decided to develop future scenarios for Sunergie. We interviewed various experts and lateral thinkers and made an overview of the most important and impactful external developments to Sunergie. Some of them were legislative and regulatory in nature. The energy transition is high on the Dutch national government's agenda. Other developments pertained to technology, such as hydrogen as an energy carrier and advances in large-scale energy storage. There were also some important shifts in the supply chain of materials and distribution channels to the consumer.

Based on several analyses and discussions we arrived at the conclusion that two key uncertainties were most relevant to Sunergie. The first one is the scale on which energy will be stored. Will people store energy at home? Or will it be done at utility-scale? The second key uncertainty related to distribution channels. Will Sunergie's products be sold by and large by installers? Or will the online retail of them grow significantly?

Sunergie turned these key uncertainties into a scenario framework that lay the foundation for four distinct scenarios. Each scenario has its own challenges and opportunities. Being the entrepreneurs that they are, Martin and Lisa did not shy away from some big decisions. For instance, they chose to develop a direct sales approach through an online distribution channel. They regarded an online store as a future-proof opportunity to better serve the consumer market, which would also create demand for their partnered installers.

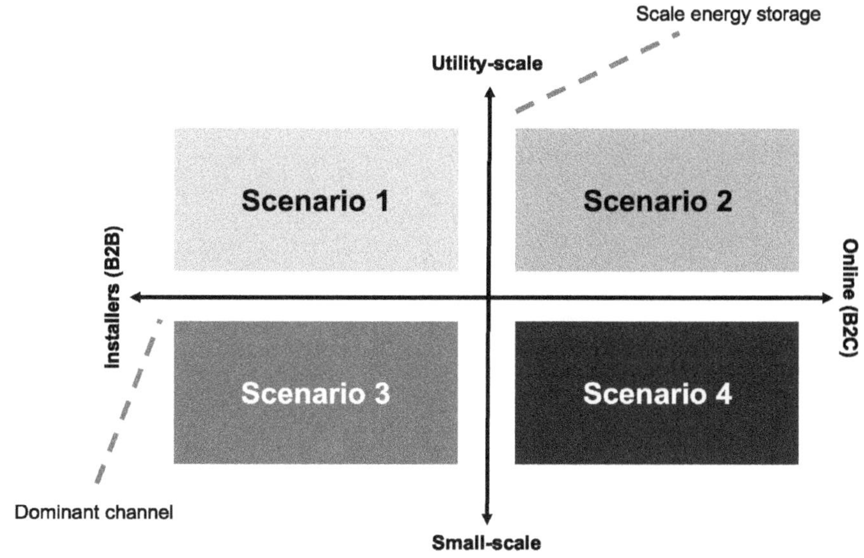

Figure 8: scenarios for Sunergie

| 24 |

5

Preparations

Perhaps the previous chapters have gotten you thinking. Perhaps you realize - like us many years ago- that you might have used some sub-optimal tools to go about certain strategic issues in the past. This is hardly surprising, as in many organizations, and many MBAs in fact, uncertainty is not, or scarcely, factored into strategic thinking. Traditional tools like business cases or extrapolation are often favored instead. Many organizations even still 'copy paste' last year's plans as a blueprint for the future.

Scenario planning, however, will help you truly appreciate the uncertainty in the external environment. But how do you actually develop and apply scenarios in practice? This book will tell you how. Yet before we do that, this chapter will first ask you whether scenario planning is the right tool for *your* job. And if so, what the objectives are that you hope to achieve with a scenario project. Once we covered that, we will go into our best practices regarding organizing a scenario project, even how to execute it in only 1 week. In the Annex of this book, and also digitally, you will find useful templates for the preparation of a scenario project.

Is scenario planning required?

Let us be clear. As enthusiastic as we might be regarding the method and its many uses, scenarios are a means and certainly not an end in themselves. Whether scenario planning is the right decision-making tool for *your* specific situation is therefore a relevant question. The answer is not always a clearcut 'yes'. In the brilliant book *20/20 Foresight* Courtney, Kirkland, and Viguerie [1997] luckily provided us with a framework that can be of assistance. In their book, these scientists explain how to match the right decision-making tool with how dynamic and unpredictable the external environment regarding a specific topic is.

Three levels of uncertainty

Courtney and his colleagues start by describing how complex and dynamic one's external environment often can be. They encourage us to always properly analyze the level of uncertainty related to a specific topic. By doing this, you can determine whether the topic you wish to explore needs to be regarded in light of a first, second, or third level of uncertainty. We will now briefly explain these three levels.

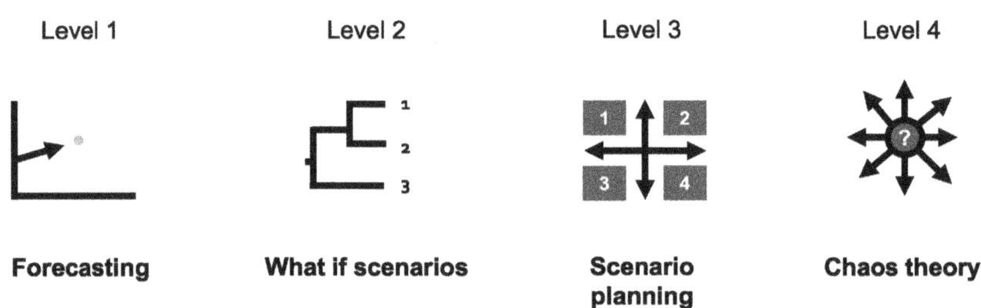

Figure 9: levels of uncertainty and decision-making tools (Courtney, et al)

Level one uncertainty

If there is a relatively stable external environment, in which there is little uncertainty and unpredictability, we speak of level one. One could say that in this case the organization's external environment is adequately stable in order to make fairly accurate predictions of the future within a pretty narrow bandwidth. For instance, imagine the distribution strategy for a chain selling hearing aids. If HQ considers opening new stores, they could quite easily calculate the risks associated with this decision. Based on regional demographic data one could rather simply calculate how many seniors would require hearing aids and what market share could be feasible. Additionally, the risks of operating new stores can contractually be minimized. No scenarios are necessary for reaching a decision.

Level two uncertainty

If the specter of one dominant uncertainty haunts a certain topic, then one can speak of level two uncertainty. This one uncertainty can have major consequences for the organization's strategy. A prime example of uncertainty that can upset a hitherto stable industry or market is changing government regulations. Radical shifts in environmental or market regulation rules, for instance. What should you do if you want to make a significant investment in a product or a company and such an uncertainty is in play? In that case 'what- if' scenarios are the right tool for the job, Courtney advises. Organizations can explore the impact of two alternative outcomes of this dominant uncertainty and use that to determine or calculate how effective their current strategy is in both scenarios.

Level three uncertainty

Especially when looking at a more distant planning horizon, many organizations are faced with level 3 uncertainty. This occurs when there are multiple uncertainties that can impact the issue at hand. Often multiple trends and uncertainties will interact, and reinforce or weaken the others, making it difficult to develop a precise picture of the future.

In situations of level three uncertainty, scenario planning is the recommended tool. Sunergie, for instance, is faced with trends and uncertainties from many different perspectives.

Level 4 uncertainty

In their book Courtney and colleagues also go into level four uncertainty. They conclude that this often is merely a temporary state that quickly shifts towards level 3. Additionally, we believe that the inherent complexity of chaos theory only needlessly complicates strategic decision making and therefore is of very limited use in most cases.

What do you want out of a scenario planning project?

When you have concluded that scenario planning is a proper tool for your specific case, you can start preparing the project. For a good project design, it is important to carefully consider what the goal of such a project is. Is the objective to stress-test the company's strategy? Do you want to identify external risks? Are you about to decide on a large investment? Or do you simply seek inspiration for innovation? Perhaps your goals might not be all that concrete and you just want to use scenarios as a tool for having a proper strategic conversation with your management team or with your most important stakeholders.

Depending on your objectives you will choose which questions will be focused on, which themes or topics are in or out of scope, and which people should contribute to the project.

Creating buy-in

An important question when designing a scenario planning project is whether the endeavor will only have a functional objective or will also be undertaken to create support and buy-in for decisions. In other words, is it solely about the destination or is the journey equally important? In the first case, expert scenarios will usually suffice; only experts on the specific topic will provide their input. In the second case – creating buy-in- it will be important to carefully identify relevant stakeholders and include them at logical moments in developing and discussing the scenarios. Scenarios are a powerful tool to explore the future with your stakeholders, either internal or external. The common frame of reference scenarios provide will make decision-making more transparent and, in doing so, create more buy-in.

Who and what will I need?

Alright, so you want to start a scenario planning project and you have formulated a concrete objective. For example, you want to generate strategic options *and* you want to include stakeholders in the process. You can now start preparing the project. Scenario planning projects can differ widely in terms of their level of detail and their time frames. You can have an inspiring and informative one-day scenario session, but you could also easily take half a year developing them. We are rather charmed by the idea of developing them in a week. In a week you can achieve the right balance between adequate detail and pace. If you prepare the project well and mobilize a dedicated team, then executing a scenario project in a week is certainly feasible.

The team

One of the first things to consider in the preparations is the assembly of a good scenario team. That is easier said than done, as many different skills are needed in the team. For starters, it is important to mobilize people with relevant expertise. People with a lot of industry knowledge and who have a good overview of the major trends and developments will form the core of the team. It is important to ensure that their points of view do not reinforce one another too much because that can result in tunnel vision. The best scenario teams therefore include people with different points of view and some lateral thinkers as well. We also recommend including people from different business or organizational units in order to shed light on the possible impact of external developments across the entire organization.

Once you got the expertise of the team covered, then it is time to take a look at specific skills you want within the team. Important examples are, a good process manager who can systematically guide the team through the process step by step, a good analyst who loves to make various analyses, and a creative thinker, who is able to visualize and vividly communicate the scenarios.

Decision making

In some cases an executive can be part of the scenario team. If this is not the case, it is important to ensure that lines of communication to 'c-level' are short. In the end, they bear ultimate responsibility and will have to make choices that emerge from the scenario project. Additionally, it can be relevant to include other organizational bodies, such as a supervisory board, employee representative bodies, and/or other important stakeholders. Many industries have specific governance codes prescribing who to include in strategy formulation and who, ultimately, formally approves or ratifies strategic choices.

Apart from their possible role in the decision-making process, a scenario project can be a great way to let various stakeholders contribute their ideas. Supervisory board members, employee representatives, staff, or external stakeholders can easily be asked to collaborate. Trend brainstorm workshops or sessions in which you will explore the implications of the scenarios are most suited for this. For those who have a decision-making role, the benefit of participating is that it will help them more easily assess the choices presented to them.

Tools

A good scenario team needs to cooperate well. In an intensive process, the team will develop four narratives outlining completely different possible futures. This is difficult without face-to-face meetings. Yet, it can be wise to make use of online tools to supplement physical meetings. Not only are generic tools available to cooperate online but there are also specific online scenario planning tools. Google a phrase like 'social scenario planning' and you will surely find a great tool. An online scenario tool can be a great addition to team meetings or workshops. Everybody can contribute simultaneously, give input 24/7, and preliminary results or deliverables can be shared so people can enrich it with additional input. All of this, without group dynamics and domineering personalities coming into play. An online tool ensures that everybody can contribute and be heard. It enables ideas and insights to be shared that otherwise might not have seen the light of day during physical workshops or meetings.

What does a 1-week program look like?

Well begun is half done, as they say. Therefore, it is important to design a good program and to choose an inspiring location. Start planning well in advance so the required facilities are still available and calendars have not filled up. At the end of this chapter, we have included an example of a program with which to run a scenario project in one week. In the next chapters we will discuss the steps in more detail.

Monday

When you follow the 1-week program, you will define the scenario scope on Monday. You will do this with the scenario team. If you have a 'sponsor' or superior, such as an executive or supervisory board member, who you might need to include, you can do so. This can be important to avoid any misunderstanding concerning the objectives of the project, the focal question, or the boundaries of the scenarios.

Tuesday

Tuesday is all about looking outward and forward. The goal is to identify as many external developments as possible. In addition to a session with the team, you might want to brainstorm with stakeholders or conduct (online) expert interviews. If this is the case, then you will need to reserve time in their schedules well in advance.

Wednesday

Analyses will fill up your Wednesday. You will assess the impact and uncertainty of external developments and, perhaps, will perform a cross-impact analysis. The goal is to arrive at a scenario framework based on the most important key uncertainties. This you will mostly do with the scenario team.

Thursday

On Thursday you need to unleash the creativity of your team. You and the team will write scenarios. The external developments you have identified and analyzed on Tuesday and Wednesday will form some of the most important ingredients for this. On this day, consider inviting some outside expertise to the team, like an illustrator or a copy writer. Of course, you need to invite them in advance.

Friday

On this final day of the program, the scenarios will have been written. Now the team will think about the implications of the scenarios you have developed the previous day. Depending on the objectives of the program, the team will brainstorm new ideas and strategic options, or will use the scenarios to 'stress-test' the current strategy. Scenarios are a great tool to engage large groups with. If you want to include many people, you can organize a larger scenario workshop or 'conference'.

	MONDAY	TUESDAY	WEDNESDAY	THURSDAY	FRIDAY
Goal	*Determine scope*	*Explore environment*	*Determine key uncertainties*	*Develop scenarios*	*Apply scenarios*
Preparations	Identify the team's and stakeholders' strategic questions	Collect trend reports and list interview partners	Survey in order to analyze external developments	Everything that fosters creativity	Studying scenarios and challenges
Activities	Workshop in order to formulate focal questions, time horizon, boundaries, and actors that might impact scenarios	‣ Study reports ‣ Interview experts ‣ Brainstorm session with team and stakeholders on external developments ‣ Filtering external developments on relevance	‣ Assess trends on uncertainty, impact, and causality ‣ Determine potential key uncertainties ‣ Determine scenario framework ‣ Test framework on relevance, divergence, and plausibility	‣ Workshop to develop four scenarios ‣ Logical chronology ‣ Clear situational description of target year ‣ Concrete definition of challenges per scenario	Depending on goal: ‣ Innovation workshop ‣ Strategic option workshop ‣ Testing strategic choices ‣ Testing planned investments
Results	A clear scope and brief for the team	Overview of relevant external developments	A validated scenario framework	Four inspiring scenario narratives	Inspiration, ideas, options, choices, or investment decisions

6

Step 1: Determine scope

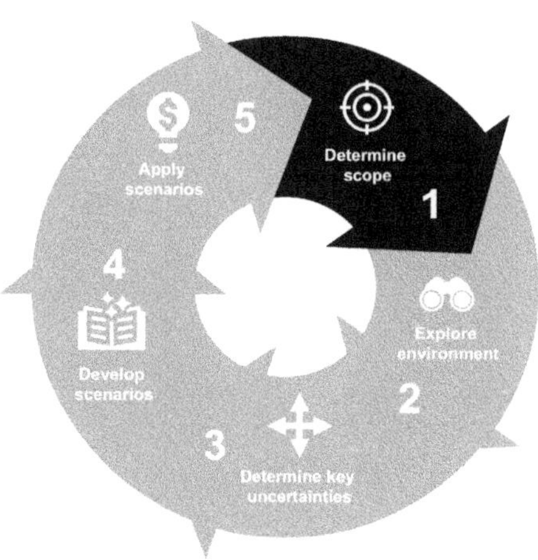

We will start this chapter with our favorite example that highlights the importance of determining the scope. Perhaps you have read *The Hitch-hiker's Guide to the Galaxy*. In this legendary book, its author, Douglas Adams, describes a futuristic intergalactic society in which the great issues of the past, such as death, war, or health, have all been solved. Most professions have been substituted by technology and many people have therefore turned to the profession of philosopher. For millennia they have been racking their brain on the answer to the ultimate question of 'life, the universe and everything'. In an attempt to come closer to an answer, they decide to build a supercomputer – Deep Thought- that has to calculate the answer. After millions of years of computing, Deep Though finally presents its answer. The answer is 42. This leaves the philosophers dumbfounded. Deep Thought explains that the answer is unknowable because the philosophers had no idea what question they actually asked.

The example of the Deep Thought supercomputer is illustrative for working with future scenarios. Scenarios are powerful instruments for organizations to explore the future and anticipate change. A supercomputer, you might say. Yet, to get concrete, relevant, and useable insights from the scenarios, it is important to ask clear questions. Scenarios that do not aim at answering clear questions regarding the future will result in generic and non-specific explorations of the future that will provide neither guidance nor assistance in taking decisions or identifying opportunities and risks. Formulating the right questions will provide the scenario project with focus, as these questions will be used throughout the process as a reference point for assessing the relevance of the scenarios and other content.

What is a scope?

A scope is much like a research question. It specifies what the scenarios will and will not explore. A good scope consists of four elements. Firstly, the *focal question*. This is a fundamental question regarding the future, which the scenario team will explore. Once you have got one, you, secondly, will determine the *time horizon*. This specifies how far ahead into the future the scenarios will peer. Thirdly, *boundaries* will define which topics or which developments are to be left out of the scenarios. Finally, it helps to have a good overview of which *actors* (stakeholders) can influence how the focal question can be answered. The golden rule in formulating the scope is that the more limited the scope is, the more focused the scenarios will be, and the better the scenarios will provide a basis for making robust and futureproof choices.

The focal question

The most important element of the scope is a focal question about the future. This focal question will provide direction and focus to the team throughout the scenario process. For instance, the focal question is important in determining which external trends and developments are relevant and which are not. It defines which topics or themes need to be addressed in the scenarios and which ones are of lesser importance. Often, one can opt for a focal question complemented with some sub-questions or themes to be included that provide more detail and specificity to the focal question.

For Sunergie the focal question was,

> " How can we maintain our position as a leading importer "
> during the energy transition?

This question should make clear that Sunergie's management worries about the company's strategic position. Sub-questions that were raised when determining the focal question were, amongst others:

- Should we reduce or expand our product offering?
- Should we strengthen our position in the value chain by cooperating more closely with installers?
- Are we big enough?
- What are opportunities for growth?

A combination of a focal question with some sub-questions always refers to uncertainty. Sunergie wants the scenarios to help provide answers to these questions.

> **How do I formulate a good focal question?**
>
> Formulating a good focal question sounds a lot easier than it is in practice. A good place for a team to start, is to think about the assumptions the organization's current strategy is based on. On which implicit expectations of the future is the strategy based? Perhaps the current strategy assumes the market to continue growing, that no new competitors will enter, that regulations or access to capital will not fundamentally change, or that the organization will possess the best production technologies. When making such underlying assumptions more explicit, the team will no doubt encounter numerous fundamental uncertainties and pose some vital questions regarding the future.

Time horizon

The second element of a scope is the time horizon. This determines how far into the future the team will look. The time horizon is always deduced from the focal question. Sunergie will have to determine how far into the future they will need to look in order to get answers on their focal question of how they can remain being a leading importer during the energy transition.

Based on their focal question and sub-questions, Sunergie chose **2030** to be the time horizon. Back in 2020 this meant that the time horizon was ten years. One of the main considerations was that the energy transition will have taken on some form or another over the next ten years. If Sunergie would have chosen a shorter time horizon, let us say five years ahead, there would be a chance that fundamental changes cannot be captured by the scenarios. Of course, when you look ten years ahead more change can occur than when looking five years ahead. Looking further ahead than ten years is also possible but runs the risk of the scenarios becoming too abstract, which makes them less useable for basing concrete decisions on.

A helpful tool in considering the time horizon for a set of scenarios is to determine what kind of choices the focal question can lead to and what their payback period might be. In the case of Sunergie issues are importing new products and changing distribution channels. These are not decisions with a short-term payback period. Therefore, it is important that the scenarios will help in assessing the relevance of such choices in the long term. In figure 10 we have listed some examples of planning horizons relating to various choices or external uncertainties. It goes without saying that a fashion retailer who needs to invest in next year's collection will look less far ahead than an institutional real estate investor or a manufacturer considering building a plant in a new market.

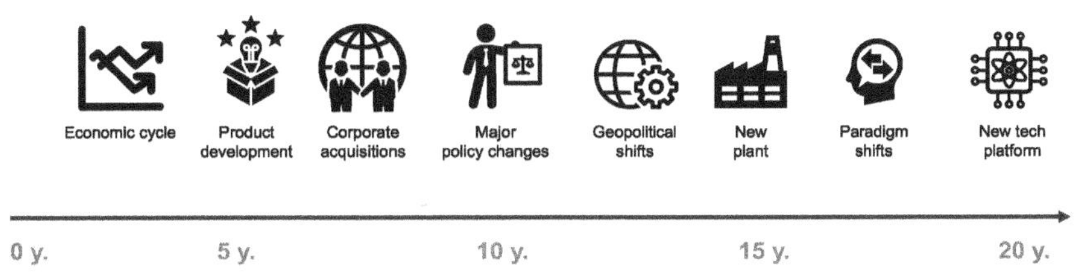

Figure 10: planning horizon per issue

Choosing the right time horizon is a crucial step in scenario planning. It will, for instance, determine which trends will be included or not in the scenarios and what their impact will be. At the same time, it is also important to realize that choosing a time horizon many years from now does not mean that you can postpone important decisions. Actually, it can be quite the opposite. Scenarios are an unrivalled tool for making timely decisions. Through exploring future uncertainties, scenarios can provide more comfort in deliberating decisions that without scenario planning would not even be contemplated.

Boundaries

You might be surprised about the fact that we pay so much attention to determining a proper scope. The reason is that with over a hundred of scenario projects under our belt we have learned that the scope determines the success of a project. Our rule of thumb is, the more concrete the scope, the more concrete the results of the scenario project will be. In addition to a good focal question, relevant and coherent sub-questions, and a fitting time horizon, the scope can be made more concrete by determining some boundaries.

These boundaries can apply to numerous topics. For instance, will the scenarios explore only the future of your national market or also foreign markets? Will you look at one product group or multiple? One industry, or multiple? Will you look at the consumer (B2C) or business to business (B2B) market? You get the idea. In determining the proper boundaries it is important to constantly ask yourself where the prospect of change and uncertainty is biggest. If the B2B market is wildly unpredictable and the B2C is not, then focus on B2B. If there are no immediate plans to enter foreign markets or if foreign revenues are marginal, then restrict the scope to the domestic market.

Naturally, Sunergie had similar discussions. One important question while defining the boundaries was whether the scenarios should cover the entire value chain or just importing activities. The underlying issue was the question whether Sunergie should manufacture solar panels themselves. Management quickly concluded that the scale and capital required was not realistic for a company like Sunergie. Therefore, production was labeled 'out of scope'. Another boundary set by the siblings was the focus on the domestic market. Neither of them had any ambition to expand internationally. Aside from those two boundaries, no further ones were formulated. Their goal was to develop a rather complete picture of the future Dutch energy landscape and what this would mean for the role of importers.

Actors

Once you have landed on a good focal question, a clear time horizon, and adequate boundaries, the next, and final, element of the scope is identifying relevant actors. With these we do not mean participants who need to be included in the project (see Chapter 5) but actors who can influence the focal question. In other words, who have an important role in shaping the explored futures. Common examples are customers, suppliers, competitors, investors, and governments. These are actors whose behaviors and preferences can determine the course of the future(s). Therefore, we recommend taking a bit of time to consider future behavior, policies, or strategies of various actors. In some cases, behavior or preferences of a certain actor can even be a key uncertainty (e.g., will the government restrict or relax certain regulations, will consumers prefer quality or low costs, etc.).

Sunergie's management team concluded that the following actors should play a role in their scenarios:

- Governments (local, regional, national)
- Consumers (businesses, households)
- Installers
- Energy companies
- Grid/distribution companies
- Banks and investors
- Large real estate and construction companies
- Solar panel and battery manufacturers

Sunergie's scenario team will therefore have to analyze the (anticipated) behavior and considerations of these actors for relevant developments.

For example, what are trends in investor behavior relating to the energy transition?

The scope workshop

Now you know which elements constitute a scope. But how do you develop a scope for your own project? Many approaches are possible, but we have the best experiences with a scope workshop with the scenario team.

Preparation

The road to good outcomes is shortest with the proper preparation. The team could, for instance, opt for collecting strategic questions from relevant people in advance of the workshop. A great aid in doing this is to ask people the oracle question:

> **Oracle question**
>
> If I were an all-knowing oracle who knows the future of our company and you were allowed to ask me one single question about the future, what would you ask?

This oracle question often results in numerous relevant questions. Does our company still exist? Will our new product have proven successful? Have regulations changed? Will fossil fuels still be used? Have we expanded? Oracle questions often are quite fundamental and related to significant uncertainties. During the workshop, the team can categorize the questions and boil them down to key themes that need to be included in the scenarios. The most dominant theme can serve as the basis for the focal question. Other relevant themes can be included as sub-questions.

An additional method to prepare the scope workshop is to analyze the current strategy or the business model (canvas) of the organization. The team will then have to determine what the underlying assumptions about the future are that underpin the strategy. Such an exercise always generates fundamental questions about these assumptions. Is the customer still willing to buy through an intermediary (installer)? Will the customer buy distinct products, or will she want 'one stop shop' solutions? These are some of the questions that came to the fore when the Sunergie team analyzed the company's current strategy.

The workshop

After a proper preparation it is time to convene with the scenario team. Take at least three hours to arrive at a good scope. It will help to make use of a template with the four elements of the scope. In the annex of this book, and digitally, we have included one.

A good place to start is to write down the strategic questions you have collected on post-its. You can cluster/group these, and post them on a large, printed template. This will give you a good impression of the most important themes. You can then try to summarize the most important themes into a focal question. The rest can potentially serve as sub-questions. Agreeing on a good focal question is not as easy as it might sound. In our experience questions starting with 'how' or 'what' are often the best. For instance, 'What will our business model look like in five years?' or 'How can we adapt to a changing society?'

Once you have landed on a focal question, you will let that guide you in further completing the scope. What is a proper time horizon based on the focal question? Use the sub-questions to set boundaries and narrow down the scope. With the focal question, time horizon, and boundaries in mind you can then identify the most relevant actors. In figure 11 you will find the results of Sunergie's workshop.

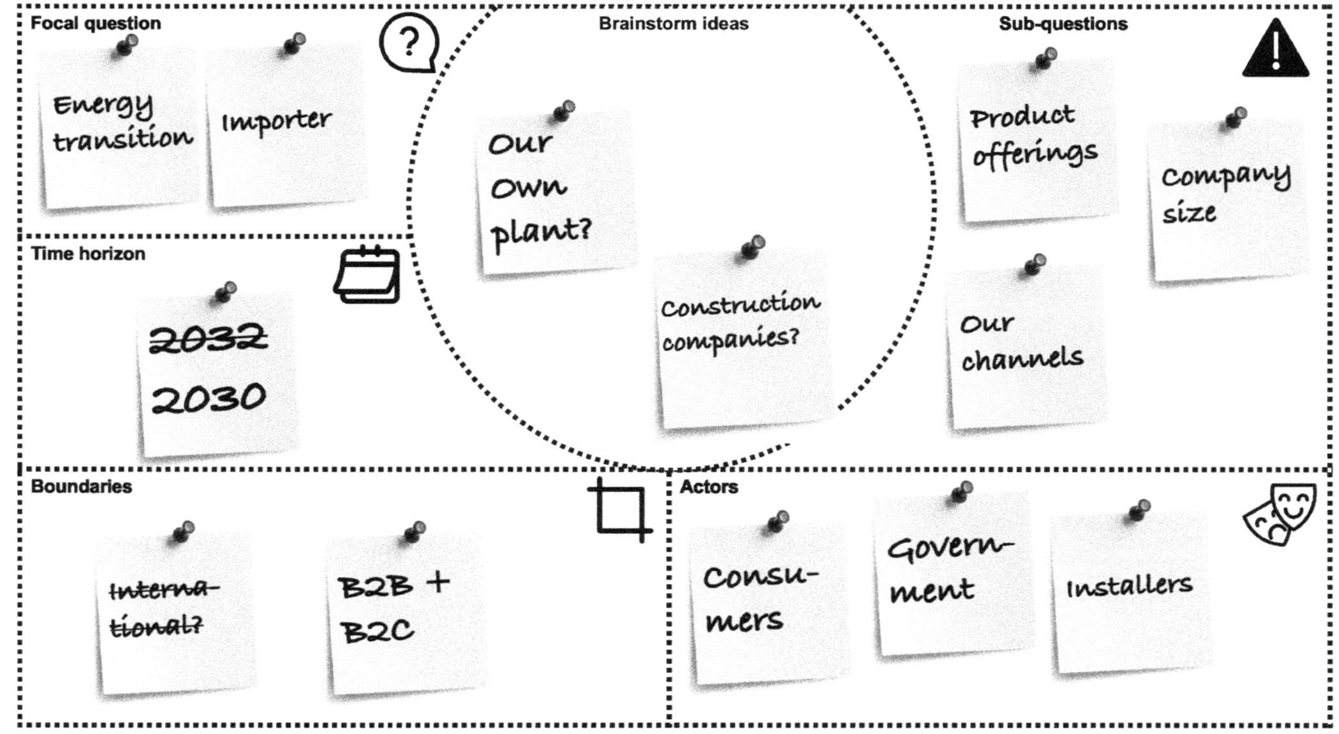

Figure 11: Sunergie's scope workshop brainstorm results

Golden rules

1. **Choose one focal question**. A common mistake is to formulate multiple focal questions. In case there is a wide range of questions (for instance, pertaining to very different markets, products, or regions), it is better to develop multiple sets of scenarios.

2. **Choose a time horizon between five and fifteen years into the future**. This ensures that the target year is not too distant, not too near. A lot can change in this time frame but also not everything. This ensures the scenarios are sufficiently concrete to use for decision-making.

3. **Focus and restrict where possible**. Keep in mind that the more concrete and focused the scope is, the more concrete and focused the scenarios will be. This will make them more effective to base decisions on.

7

Step 2: Explore the external environment

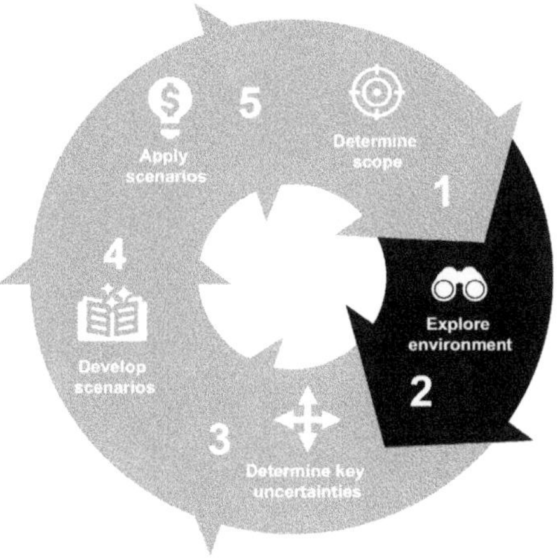

When, at the start of this century, we started to advise organizations on long-term planning, the instrument of scenario planning was far from popular. We were still living in the era that Harvard economist James Stock dubbed the 'Great Moderation'. This era lasted from the 80s of the previous century until the financial crisis of 2007-2008. That era was characterized by low inflation, steady economic growth, and the waning awareness of uncertainty in the minds of decision-makers. It would often take us dozens of PowerPoint slides and many examples to convince people that the external environment is unpredictable by nature and that disregarding this fact can exact a heavy toll on organizations.

The past couple of years, however, only a few slides would suffice. During the last two decades we have witnessed a dotcom bubble, two worldwide pandemics, a global financial crisis, the Arab Spring, Trump in the White House, a nuclear disaster, Brexit, and a war in Europe. And with this we might have seen only a glimpse of what is yet to come. The war in Ukraine has ushered in new uncertainties, not just in terms of geopolitics and military conflict but also relating to trade and access to resources and commodities. Across the globe issues like scarcities, inflation, wealth redistribution, new social divides, the impact of technology, sustainability, and climate change will leave their mark. The question therefore is, will we stand idly by? Or will we spring into action by recognizing trends and signposts in time and adapting to these by generating new ideas and business models?

The external environment

Does your partner also sometimes tell you not to worry about things you cannot control? This might be great advice for your personal life but not so much for organizations. Every organization is an open system; a system that interacts with the outside world. In other words, the external environment. This external environment is a complex system in itself, comprised of various trends, uncertainties, and behaviors that are outside the direct sphere of influence of an individual organization. The developments in their external environment can make or break organizations. A pretty good reason, therefore, to explore it in more detail.

In this second step of the scenario planning project, you will explore the external environment in order to identify relevant developments and shed light on their impact. Once you have determined the scope of the scenario analysis, you will systematically investigate which factors can exert an influence on the focal question and sub-questions you listed earlier in the scope. When we say systematic, we mean that, almost like with an onion, you will peel off the external environment layer by layer.

Macro environment

If the external environment is an imaginary onion, then the outer layer is the macro environment. This layer is relevant for every organization, regardless of industry or business model. The macro environment is the domain of political dynamics, of economic cycles, ecological issues, technological developments, socio-cultural shifts, and demographic patterns. In order to systematically examine the macro environment, you can use the PESTED model. This is an acronym for Political, Economic, Social, Technological, Ecological, and Demographic factors. When you use this model to guide your exploration, you can be fairly sure you will have a complete picture of the macro environment.

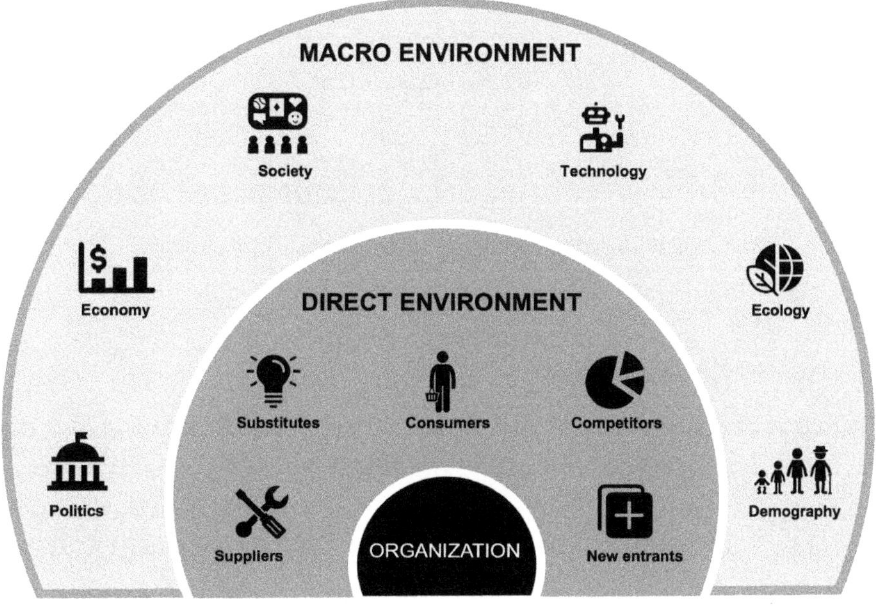

Figure 12: the layers of the external environment

You can use various methods in exploring the macro environment. Often, there is a lot of information you can collect from publicly available sources, such as research reports, but you can also opt for expert interviews. In order to get a complete picture, Sunergie's scenario team decided to organize a brainstorm with experts from both within and outside of their industry. The results you can find in table 2.

Dimension	Developments
Political	• Increasing fragmentation of parties • Increasing international regulation concerning energy and climate
Economic	• Increasing economic volatility • Increasing reshoring • From ownership to access
Social	• Increasing polarization • Increasing inequality of opportunities • Rise of bottom-up and grassroots initiatives • Shift towards self-reliance
Technological	• Growing impact of big data • Increasing automation and robotization • Electrification of mobility
Ecological	• Increasing demand for sustainability • More noticeable effects of climate change • Increasing resource scarcity • Increasing popularity of low consumption lifestyles
Demographic	• Ageing population • Increasing urbanization • Fleeing to the countryside out of the big cities

Table 2: macro environment brainstorm results Sunergie

The direct environment

When you explore the external environment, it is important to identify as many developments as possible and forego inferring conclusions concerning their impact at this stage. For now, you want to ensure the list of developments is as exhaustive and complete as possible. Try to also avoid the pitfall of disregarding 'weak signals'. Often such weaker signals and hard to define developments can point you towards a relevant nascent trend. Often, the opinions or behaviors of a small socio-economic *avant garde* can become mainstream over time. Quitting smoking, not eating animal proteins, or flight shaming are some examples of such developments.

In order to get the fullest possible picture of the external environment, you will also need to explore the direct environment of the organization in addition to the macro environment.

Our cognitive biases distort our perception

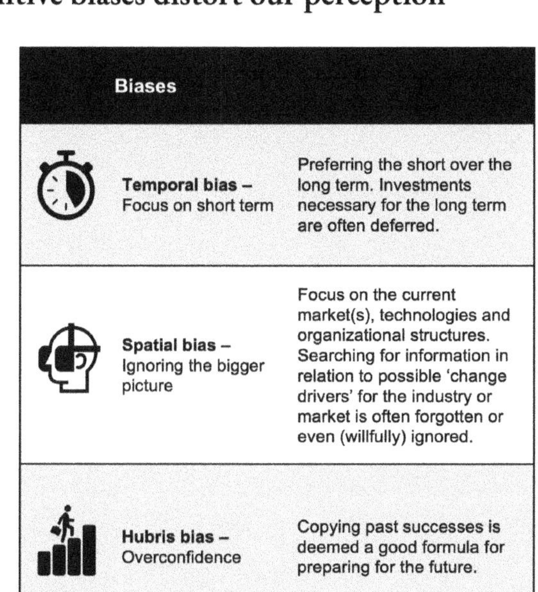

(Levinthal & March)

When analyzing the external environment, it is important to be aware that we are only human. Every person has their own filters and biases that can distort their perception. Levinthal and March wrote about this in their influential article 'The Myopia of Learning'. The authors provide an overview of common myopias (our biases) that cause us to incorrectly process information. The most important ones are the temporal, spatial, and hubris myopias. The temporal myopia causes us to prioritize the short over the long term when we filter information. The spatial

> myopia is the reason why we often prefer existing structures and behaviors, making it hard for us to imagine these changing. The hubris myopia predisposes us to regard past lessons and insights (and our successes) as indicative for the future. For every scenario team it is important to be aware of these pitfalls and to challenge each other on these when members suspect tunnel vision looms.

For companies the direct environment often consists of clients, competitors, products, substitutes, suppliers, and partners. For public organizations it often entails stakeholders, such as citizens, governments, companies, and civil society organizations.

Sunergie opted to analyze its direct environment by means of a *five forces analysis* (Porter). The scenario team chose to combine a survey amongst suppliers with a brainstorm session with a panel of employees and external visionaries. In light of the confidential nature of the session, suppliers and competitors were not invited. The results of their exploration of their direct environment can be found in table 3.

Dimension	Developments
Customers	• More online shopping for total energy solutions • Increasing demand for convenience • Electrification of energy
Suppliers	• Decreasing supply security from China • Increasing vertical integration
Competitors	• Increase of mergers and acquisitions (scale) • Increasing vertical integration
New entrants	• More (foreign) B2C competitors • Increase of competitors from outside our industry
Substitutes	• Increasing use of hydrogen as energy carrier • Rise of utility scale energy storage

Table 3: developments in Sunergie's direct environment

Stakeholder behavior

For most issues a good exploration of the macro and direct environments will provide you with a complete picture of the dynamics of the external environment. However, for some issues uncertainty might be even a bit closer to home. Sometimes there might be uncertainty regarding the behavior of shareholders, or that of employees. In case the behavior of important stakeholders might have a big impact and is not within the control of the organization itself, it will be relevant to identify possible behaviors and to include these in the scenario analysis.

The external developments workshop

Now you know which elements constitute the external environment, but how do you arrive at a compact and useable overview of the most relevant developments? To do that, it is crucial to have a well-prepared workshop in which external developments are identified and subsequently clustered into a logical overview.

Preparations

As with any workshop, a good preparation will lead to the best results. In order to have a successful workshop, it is important to not only develop a good program but also to collect good input. External developments can be found in various sources. Desk research, for instance, can already provide valuable insights. Many renowned thinktanks, advisory firms, or magazines publish an annual overview of megatrends. For instance, *The Economist* has their annual 'The World in' series. Industry associations, investment banks, and accountancy firms often publish insightful industry reports.

In addition to desk research, it can be of great value to interview several experts and visionaries. These could be people that know your industry inside and out, but they can also be people with fresh perspectives from a different industry, academia, or even a foreign competitor. Face-to-face interviews always result in a wealth of information but if you are working within a short timeframe then you could also consider blogs and vlogs of visionaries.

Finally, in preparation of the workshop, you can also opt for organizing multiple panel discussions with customers or researchers/academics. During such panel discussions you can both identify relevant external developments and collect input on what the implications of those might be on your organization or industry.

The workshop

When you have prepared the workshop, it is time to get together and run it with the team. Take at least three hours to properly identify developments and cluster them into a compact overview, which is called a *trend complex*. We have good experience with sessions using a template on which participants can post their input and then cluster them. Such a template can be found in the Annex of this book or as a download.

If you use the template, participants will first have to write what they regard as important developments on post-its. Then they can be posted (within the relevant dimension) on the template one by one. Very similar developments or those that are highly interconnected can be grouped together. Various clusters of external developments will no doubt start to appear. The next step is to give a clear and unambiguous name to these clusters. This way, it should be clear what is meant by that cluster. If you suspect that some developments are missing, you can organize an additional brainstorm session. Sunergie also had a brainstorm session with their team. The PESTED results of their session you can find in figure 13.

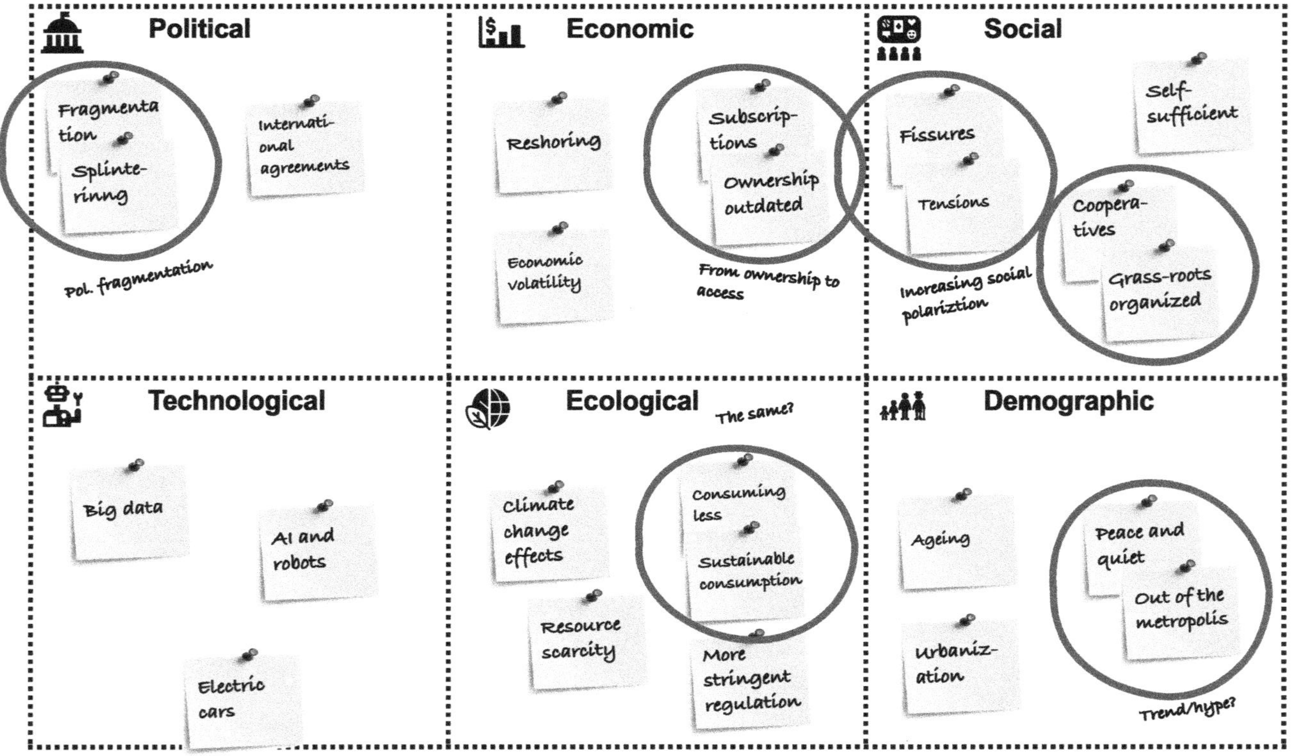

Figure 13: results of macro environment brainstorm session Sunergie

Golden rules

1. **Use multiple research methods**. Try to combine desk research, expert interviews, and workshops. That way you can compile a complete overview of developments with enough attention to weak signals that could usher in change.
2. **Cluster developments.** Sometimes identifying developments can lead to a list of over a hundred of them. This is undesirable in light of the next step in the process, analyzing those external developments. Therefore, it is important to cluster developments into a compact overview. In practice, reducing everything down to a 'net' list of approximately fifteen to twenty clusters is often achievable. This is a workable number of developments for subsequent analyses.
3. **Describe the developments.** It is important to - at least briefly - describe the clustered external developments. This will ensure that everybody on the team works with the same definitions and no misunderstandings will occur. If not done properly, we have seen people work with completely different interpretations of the same development.

8

Step 3: Determine key uncertainties

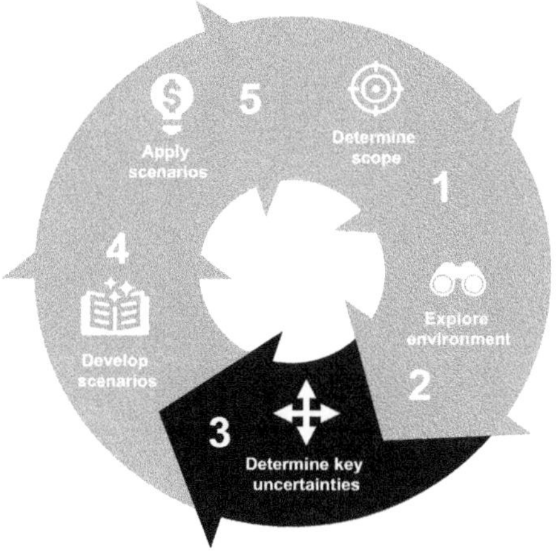

Now you have arrived at the third step of scenario planning, determining the key uncertainties. This is the most fundamental step but also the most counter-intuitive one. We humans are hardwired to look for certainties, not uncertainties, when making decisions. Our brain has difficulties dealing with uncertainties and that can cause some major issues. A common reaction to uncertainty is *denial*. When it is hard to interpret information, for instance, when we perceive only few certain and predictable elements, we subconsciously decide to disregard uncertainty and pretend it does not exist. A common practice we encounter in many business cases.

Truth be told, the opposite can be equally problematic. A human being simply cannot account for each and every possibility and uncertainty. Considering every possible uncertainty in decision-making can lead to *paralysis*. It is a bit like the donkey in French philosopher's Buridan's parable, in which a (rational) donkey cannot choose between an equally appealing stack of hay and a bucket of water, and ultimately dies of both starvation and thirst due to his indecision. Both denial and paralysis are, of course, undesirable. Both lead to bad decisions. With scenario planning you try to find the middle ground by looking for the key uncertainties underneath an issue. The key uncertainties are fundamental uncertainties that not only have a direct influence on the topics in your scope but can also set the entire system of external developments, the *trend complex* (see previous chapter), in motion. Therefore, they form the basis of scenarios and the inferences these will contain.

Key uncertainties

Have you ever played dominoes as a kid? You could regard the most important external developments as domino stones. The key uncertainties would in that case be the first in a row. When these fall, all the others will fall too. Key uncertainties can vary in character and origin but are always fundamental. For instance, climate change, technological standards or developments, (social) value systems, or geopolitical changes. Tables 4 and 5 list some key uncertainties that we have come across frequently in recent years.

Perspective		Common key uncertainties
	Political	• The degree to which the world is 'open' • The degree of political fragmentation • The degree of liberalization
	Economic	• The transition from ownership to access • Increasing scarcity of resources • The end of the 'growth' paradigm
	Social	• From shareholder to stakeholder value • The degree of segregation in society • Increasing polarization
	Technological	• The adoption of new technologies • Labor substitution by new technologies • Ethical outlook on adopting new technologies
	Ecological	• The speed of global warming • Level of sustainability ambitions • Degree of global cooperation on emissions reduction
	Demographic	• Increase of refugees • Degree of urbanization • Level of impact of infectious diseases on population

Table 4: common key uncertainties (macro environment)

Perspective		Common key uncertainties
	Customers	• Increasing demand for full-service • Increasing price sensitivity
	Suppliers	• Increasing competitive pressure • Competitors increasing production capacity
	Competitors	• Rise of new business models • Entrants from outside of the industry
	New entrants	• Downstream vertical integration • New alliances and partnerships
	Substitutes	• Rise of technological substitutes • Rise of new ways of working

Table 5: common key uncertainties (direct environment)

Identifying key uncertainties for a set of scenarios is a two-round process. In the first round you will filter the trend complex for potential key uncertainties. In the second round you will choose the two key uncertainties that will form the framework for your scenarios.

Potential key uncertainties

In order to filter out key uncertainties from the trend complex, we use three filters:

1. Impact
2. Uncertainty
3. Causality

A possible key uncertainty has much impact on the focal question, is uncertain, and can exert its influence on many developments throughout the trend complex. We will explain the three filters in more detail shortly. Sit down, grab something to drink, or read this chapter twice, as this chapter can be a bit complex but, ultimately, illuminating nonetheless.

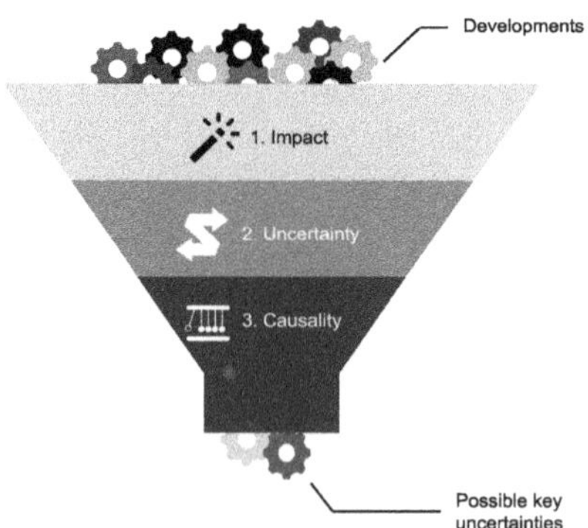

Figure 14: filters for the key
uncertainties

1. The impact filter

This filter assesses the relevance of individual external developments. How relevant are the developments that have been identified to the topics mentioned in the scope of the scenario analysis? How much potential impact can a development have on an issue or theme? We often assess each individual development on a 0-4 scale. When doing this, it is important to not only look at the focal question but to keep relevant sub-questions in mind as well. Of course, all within the time horizon and the boundaries that have been determined. Sometimes a certain development can have a really high impact but outside the in-scope time horizon, or in a different market than specified in the scope.

Sunergie's scenario team also assessed the impact of the most relevant developments. In their case, the external development of 'reshoring' did not make it through the impact filter as the topic of production location was labeled out of scope, as they previously discussed that Sunergie will remain solely an importer and not become a producer. The development of 'robotization' was also filtered out as they did not consider robots installing solar panels on roofs plausible by 2030. Perhaps a few years later, some argued. Given the fact that (centrally located) Sunergie operates throughout the entire country of the Netherlands, the development of people migrating from the urbanized west to the more rural and affordable provinces in the east was deemed less impactful. If Sunergie would have only served customers in the west of the country, then this migration development from west to east might have been deemed more impactful, as it would mean that the market in the west might shrink whereas more opportunities in the east would arise.

Once you have assessed the impact of the various developments, you can start to filter them. We always calculate the average impact score of the developments. Only those that score above average will continue to the second filter.

2. The uncertainty filter

After applying the impact filter, you probably will have reduced the number of external developments that vie for being a key uncertainty. For instance, out of an original list of twenty, fifteen might remain. Now it is important to assess the uncertainty of the remaining external developments. We now have to dig a bit deeper into the theory in order to provide the necessary context for the important step of assessing the uncertainty of developments. This is because uncertainty can apply to two elements of developments, namely (A) the progression of a development or (B) the consequences or effects of a development.

> **A. Progression.** Please think along with us. You probably will be able to think of some developments of which you are certain they will have some sort of impact. However, you might not be so sure about how quickly or intensely that will transpire. Their progression, therefore, is uncertain. Will something happen rapidly or slowly? Linear or exponential? Evolutionary or revolutionary? For example, we all know that the use of fossil fuels is finite. Many companies probably know quite well what the impact of that would be. For instance, car manufacturers will no longer make internal combustion engines, installers will no longer install gas-based heating systems, grid and utility companies will need to lay electricity cables instead of gas mains. Therefore, what such companies will need to do is quite clear. The time frame, however, might not be. Depending on numerous other variables, phasing out fossil fuels could progress quickly, but could also go rather slowly, or in fits and starts.
>
> **B. Consequences**. An external development could qualify for the predicate 'uncertain' based on its progression, but also by virtue of its consequences. Some external developments might exhibit a fairly predictable progress or tempo. However, their consequences are still up in the air. For instance, think of the

development 'increasing impact of Artificial Intelligence'. In addition to uncertainty regarding its progression, its consequences are uncertain as well. For instance, will it lead to a net reduction of jobs (net labor substitution)? Or will there be ample of new jobs and opportunities, like in previous industrial revolutions? Rival schools of thought exist on this topic, with both able to make a convincing case. Regulatory or policy changes are a common example as well. While election cycles are often easy to predict in most political systems, the leaning of a new government might be uncertain, however. For instance, will it implement stricter regulations on an industry or will it opt for deregulation? Will it be inclined to raise taxes or lower them?

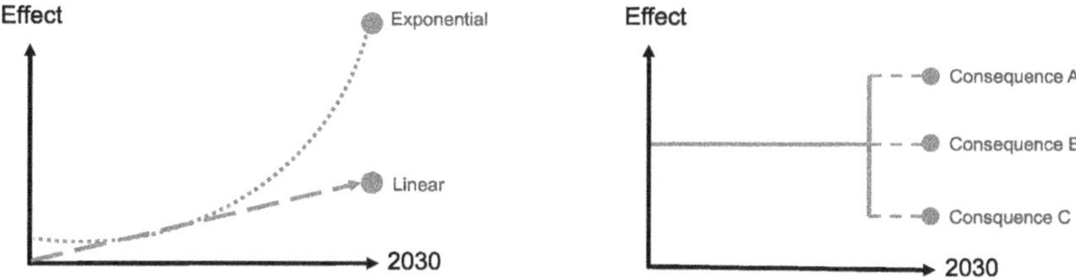

Figure 15: the difference between uncertainty regarding progression (left) and consequence (right)

Sunergie also assessed the uncertainty of the external developments on their radar. The results of this you can find in table 6. It is interesting to see how by assessing the impact and uncertainty, multiple types of developments are taking shape. We see developments that combine a high impact with a high uncertainty, such as the rise of foreign competitors catering directly to end-consumers (B2C) or the rise of utility scale energy storage. These developments are prime candidates for key uncertainties. We also see external developments combining a high impact with very little uncertainty, such as an ageing population and the increasing demand for convenience. Such developments are named 'autonomous trends'. Although they are no candidates for being a key uncertainty, they still are important to Sunergie. Given their low uncertainty (therefore, relatively high certainty), the company can - and should- respond to those trends already. Sunergie does not need scenarios to consider the impact of autonomous trends.

External Developments	Impact	Uncertainty
Increasing fragmentation of parties	2.8	2.0
From ownership to access	2.2	3.5
Shift towards self-reliance	3.1	3.0
Growing impact of big data	2.5	2.0
Increasing demand for sustainability	3.0	2.5
Ageing population	3.0	0.2
Fleeing to the countryside (out of the big cities)	1.2	3.5
Increasing use of hydrogen as energy carrier	3.8	3.3
Rise of utility scale energy storage	3.8	3.3
More online shopping for total energy solutions	3.3	3.2
More (foreign) B2C competitors	3.2	3.0
Increasing demand for convenience	2.8	1.8
Average	**2.8**	**2.8**

Table 6: impact and uncertainty external developments for Sunergie (scale 0-4)

3. The causality filter

Still bearing with us? Looking for potential key uncertainties certainly is not the most exciting and creative aspect of a scenario analysis. However, it is one of the most fundamental ones. So far, we have assessed the external developments' impact and their uncertainty. Many scenario planning books or practitioners stop the analysis here. They claim key uncertainties combine a high impact with high uncertainty. True as that is, it is far from the complete picture. A proper key uncertainty also is a proper *change driver*. By looking at causality amongst the developments you can distinguish between developments that are root causes for change and those that can be deemed a result/effect of change. In other words, which are developments that can be regarded the first domino stone tipping the other ones over?

Then what exactly is the difference between root causes and results? For instance, consider external developments such as 'increasing unemployment' and 'economic downturn'. Or 'more stringent environmental and emission laws' and the 'electrification of cars'. Or 'increasingly unequal access to economic and social opportunities' and 'polarization of society'. For each of these three pairs you probably almost instantaneously have an idea which one leads to the other. An economic downturn leads to unemployment and not the other way around. Strict emission and environmental laws significantly speed up the uptake of electric vehicles. Unequal social and economic opportunities lead to a polarized society. Developments that have a big causal impact on all the other developments on the list can be root causes - or drivers- of change. These form a great foundation for scenarios because they offer a great causal starting point to deduce how other developments will take on different shapes and quantities in the various scenarios.

Proper key uncertainties therefore are highly impactful and uncertain but also trigger a whole causal chain of events. How do you assess that causality then, you might wonder. You can do this with a so-called *cross impact analysis*. Using a pre-defined scale (we often use 0-3), you will reason how development 1 influences development 2, how development 1 influences development 3, development 4, etc. You do this by following the rows in a matrix from left to right (see table 7). Once you have completed this, you automatically also have assessed each development's dependence. Therefore, at the end of the analysis you have a pretty clear picture of which developments have a large influence on others and which ones are very dependent on how others progress.

Let us return to Sunergie once again. In their assessment, only a few developments scored high on both impact and uncertainty. Only a few developments of those also displayed a high (above average) causality. In the abbreviated example of table 7, these are the light grey rows. The most influential developments were the rise of utility scale energy storage and online shopping becoming the dominant distribution channel.

	Increasing focus on sustainability	From ownership to access	Increasing online shopping for energy solutions	Increasing vertical integration	More new entrants from outside industry	Rise of utility scale energy storage	...	Total Causality
Increasing focus on sustainability		2	0	0	0	1	...	3
From ownership to access	0		1	2	2	1	...	6
Increasing online shopping for energy solutions	0	2		2	3	0	...	7
Increasing vertical integration	0	1	1		1	1	...	4
More new entrants from outside industry	0	1	2	2		1	...	6
Rise of utility scale energy storage	0	3	1	2	2		...	8
...	...	...	...	...	...	...		...
Total Dependence	0	8	5	7	8	4	...	

Table 7: cross-impact analysis Sunergie

Selecting the key uncertainties

The result of the analyses is an assessment of all the developments' impact, uncertainty, and causality. Developments scoring above average on all three criteria are potential key uncertainties. In our experience, often two to four developments qualify as candidates, sometimes only one. Depending on the number of scenarios you want to develop you will need to select either one (for two scenarios) or two key uncertainties (for four scenarios).

Extreme values

In most cases, organizations will want to explore third level uncertainty (see Chapter 4). This entails selecting two key uncertainties in order to develop four scenarios (see Chapter 2). The extremes – or poles- of the axes you need to label with their extreme values as you define the scenario framework (2x2 matrix). A quick word about those 'extremes'. Key uncertainties of which the nature of the uncertainty is their pace or progress, and not their consequences, often have extremes labeled as 'more' or 'less', 'fast' or 'slow', 'linear' or 'exponential'. For instance, a slow versus a fast economic recovery or linear versus exponential pace of innovation. Key uncertainties for which the nature of the uncertainty are their consequences, often have extreme labeled in terms of those consequences. For instance, geopolitical stability vs instability, strict regulation versus lax regulation, centralized vs decentralized, bricks versus clicks, etc.

Choosing from alternatives

When the analyses result in two possible key uncertainties, the scenario team will have an easy day. Unfortunately, this is seldomly the case. Often the team will have to choose from multiple key uncertainty candidates. This is not always easy but the team will get there in the end. We always do this in two steps. Firstly, there are some rules of thumb in considering which combinations will work and which ones will fail. If after this multiple frameworks still remain possible, we will test their relevance for the organization.

Our two rules of thumb are fairly simple.

1. **Independence**. The most important thing to consider is whether the key uncertainties are not too interrelated with each other. If they influence each other greatly, this will mean that some scenarios are more logical and more plausible than others. The aim

is to come up with four scenarios that are roughly equally probable. You can refer back to the cross-impact analysis to test this. A less accurate test is to see whether the two candidates are from different PESTED dimensions. If two potential key uncertainties could both be regarded as economic developments, odds are that they are too interconnected. For instance, take two economic uncertainties, employment and the economic cycle. It will be very difficult to plausibly (!) argue and imagine a world in which employment is on the rise during an economic downturn.

2. **Match with time horizon.** The second rule of thumb is a proper match with the time horizon. If you want to develop scenarios for the long term (let us say 10 or more years ahead), two macro uncertainties are your leading candidates for key uncertainties. If your scenarios have a relatively short-term focus, then choosing some more direct and industry specific developments makes a lot of sense because their impact will be noticed more quickly. If you look at the medium term, often 5-10 years, a combination of a macro and a direct uncertainty often works well.

Testing for relevance

Of course, we hope that by now you were able to select two key uncertainties for your framework. In case you have not, no worries. Now you will test which of the possible frameworks (combinations of key uncertainties) are most relevant in light of the focal question for the scenarios. Let us imagine that after all the analyses and rules of thumbs you are still left with three possible key uncertainties. This will leave you with three possible frameworks (combinations of uncertainties A-B, A-C, B-C). We always like to sketch those frameworks on a flip chart or white board and then discuss which one is the most fitting scenario framework. Is it easy to imagine each of the four futures in each framework? To keep track of it all, you can summarize the broad strokes of those worlds in bullets per quadrant. Once you have done that for every possible framework, you are ready to test them. A good scenario framework (resulting in four probable scenarios) will need to meet four criteria. The team will need to assess which of the alternatives score best on these.

1. **Relevance**. The framework should be able to give you enough relevant inspiration and information in order to answer the focal question.
2. **Divergence**. The framework should result in four radically different futures; not four variations on a theme. Extremity is what you are looking for.
3. **Plausibility**. Good scenarios are extreme, yet plausible. Can the team reasonably imagine all four scenarios possibly occurring?
4. **Challenging**. A proper framework should result in four scenarios that will challenge readers' assumptions and pictures of the future. Does it inspire them to think differently? Great scenarios need to create some friction, some unease in the readers' mind. If they are too 'comfortable' they will not challenge and inspire.

It was not easy for Sunergie's team to choose a framework. After all the analyses, three potential key uncertainties remained.

1. The rise of utility-scale energy storage
2. The rise of online shopping for energy solutions
3. Increasing use of hydrogen as energy carrier

The team first discussed the nature of the uncertainty of these three external developments. Regarding energy storage they assessed that an important element in the uncertainty was the scale. Will energy be stored rather decentralized and small-scale, like in home (or office) or neighborhood batteries? Or will large-scale, utility-scale, power-to-hydrogen or power-to-air type facilities of energy companies be dominant? The uncertainty regarding online shopping in the end was about which distribution channel customers will gravitate towards. Will future customers prefer to let an installer choose which solar panels and/or home batteries will be installed? Or will online business models take over contact with customers/end-users? The uncertainty regarding hydrogen is about the dominant energy carrier in 2030. Will everything in homes or offices be electric (heating, stoves, etc.)? Or will the natural gas infrastructure be repurposed for hydrogen?

Sunergie's team noticed in testing some frameworks that there was a lot of interdependence between the uncertainty regarding scale of energy storage and the uncertainty regarding energy carriers. Combining those two (rather technological) uncertainties therefore was ruled out. Two options then remained, a combination of scale of energy storage with distribution channel, or a combination of energy carrier with distribution channel. The main properties, the broad strokes, of the scenarios those two frameworks would produce were brainstormed in a workshop. Subsequently, the two possible frameworks were tested in terms of relevance, divergence, plausibility, and how challenging they were.

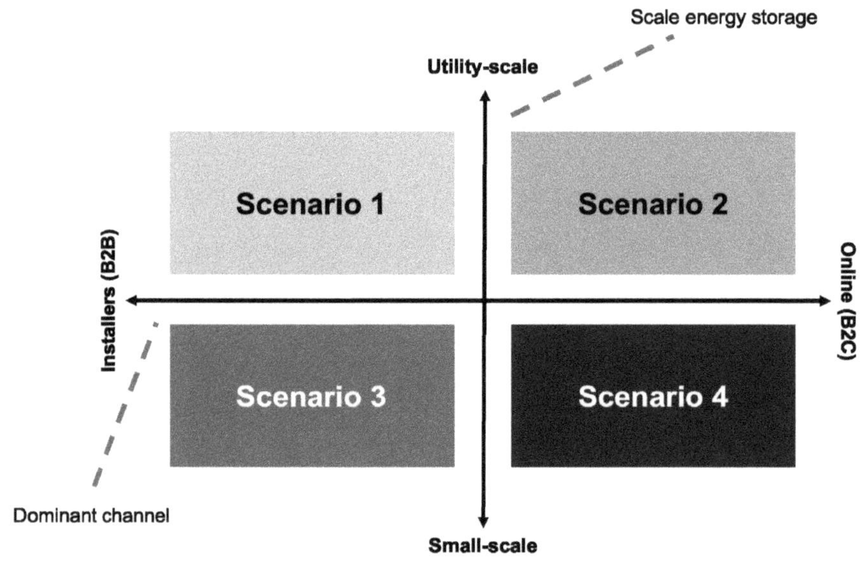

Figure 16: scenarios for Sunergie

The framework of figure 16 scored markedly higher than the others. Especially the relevance for the focal question and the plausibility of all four scenarios clinched its victory.

The key uncertainties workshop

You now know how from a 'net list' of external developments you can arrive at key uncertainties. First, you assess the impact, uncertainty, and causality of these developments. Based on two easy rules of thumb you will try to combine key uncertainties into some plausible frameworks. Then you will test these frameworks for relevance. This is quite the enterprise. You might wonder whether this is all feasible in a three-hour workshop. Fortunately, the answer is yes. Certainly with the proper preparations.

Preparations

Making use of proper templates for external development analysis and framework selection makes preparing the 'key uncertainties workshop' a whole lot easier. You can analyze the developments during the workshop, but we prefer to get that input, if possible, beforehand by means of a digital survey. In that survey, you can ask the respondents to assess the the external developments' impact on the focal question and their degree of uncertainty. We suggest accompanying that survey with a document containing brief descriptions of the developments to ensure the respondents are all on the same page regarding what they entail.

The workshop

After the proper preparations, it is time to gather the team. The workshop will consist of two parts, analysis of the external developments and key uncertainties selection.

We recommend using a template (figure 17) for analyzing the external developments. In this template you can categorize them based on their impact and uncertainty. We suggest writing down the developments on separate post-its and then arrange them according to their survey scores on the matrix. If you were unable to send out a digital survey, you can organize a 'ranking the developments' session during the workshop in which the team discusses the impact and uncertainty of the external developments and votes on their spot in the matrix. Those combining a high impact with a high uncertainty are potential key uncertainties. You will not have time to do a full cross impact analysis during the workshop. If you have 20 developments, you will have to look at (20*20)-20 causal relations, 380 in total... A good short-cut therefore is to only do a cross impact analysis on the developments that combine high impact with high uncertainty.

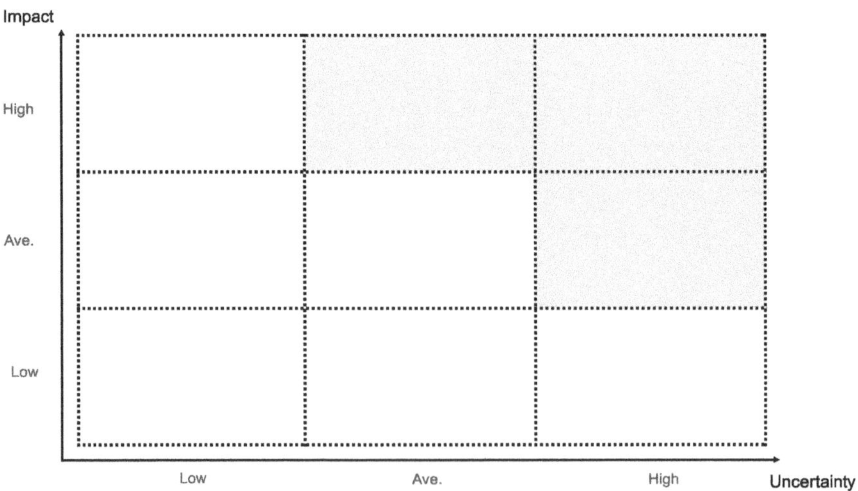

Figure 17: template for impact and uncertainty assessment

After these analyses, you are probably left with three or four key uncertainties. You can now use the template used for Figure 18 in order to brainstorm on some basic outlines of the scenarios and then test the frameworks' relevance, plausibility, divergence, and how challenging they are. For this, you can use post-its once again. Figure 18 showcases Sunergie's go at it.

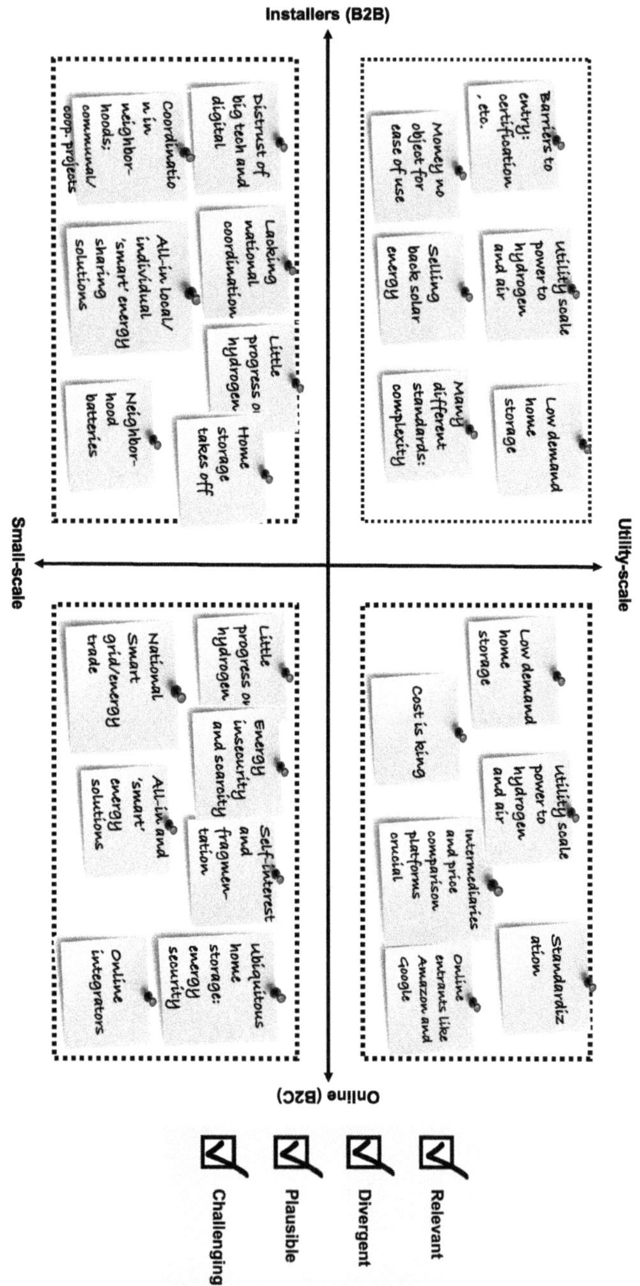

Figure 18: brainstorm Sunergie

Golden rules

1. **Causality is more important than impact**. If choosing key uncertainties is a bit problematic, then prioritize the criterion of causality over impact. Reason being that an uncertainty with a high degree of causal influence sets in motion all the other developments, which in turn could impact the focal question for the scenarios.

2. **Don't use events as an axis.** A specific event can be an important uncertainty for some organizations. Brexit or the length of the covid 19 pandemic are some recent examples. Risk of such uncertainties is that if the event goes a certain way shortly after drafting up the scenarios, half of your scenarios will be irrelevant and unusable. Two alternatives are at your disposable. The first is to look at underlying developments, for instance regarding Brexit, increasing hostility towards the EU, for instance, which can still be relevant after the event in question. The second option is to make specific 'what-if' scenarios based on that important event.

3. **Kill your darlings.** Even after applying all the rules for arriving at two proper key uncertainties, there is a (very small) chance that none of the possible frameworks meet all the criteria. For instance, not every scenario is plausible or challenging. In that case, especially if there is very little time for going back to the drawing board, it is preferable to leave out a certain scenario and develop only three plausible, relevant, divergent, and challenging scenarios instead.

| 78 |

9

Step 4: Develop scenarios

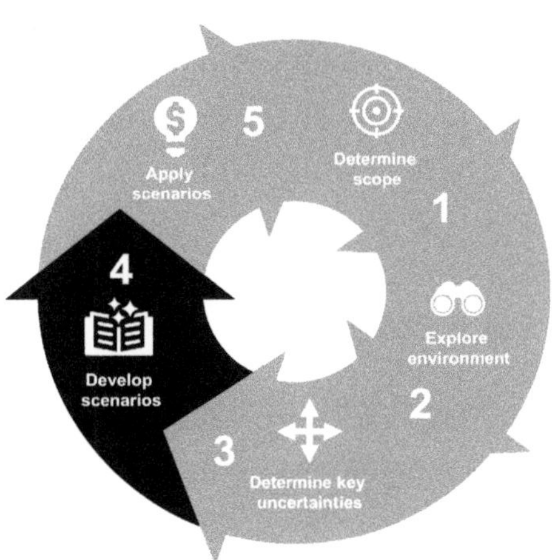

The fourth step of scenario planning is developing scenarios that are vibrant and compelling narratives of the future. Whereas identifying key uncertainties is a rather rational and methodological step, creating good scenarios is more of a creative and imaginative process. Writing scenario narratives is a rather delicate process. A process in which you will use various ingredients such as facts, expectations, opinions, and (hypothetical) examples to make coherent and plausible stories of the future. These narratives can take on several forms, ranging from prose to videos, newspapers, or infographics.

The importance of storytelling is increasingly recognized as a valuable instrument in many an MBA now. Stories are an important element in how organizations make sense of their business environment. Good, entertaining narratives can explain developments, persuade, challenge, and offer inspiration. The 'truth' or value of such stories are not so much rooted in their factual underpinnings but rather in giving meaning to events or developments that are difficult to make sense of. Former Shell strategist Arie de Geus was quick to recognize the value of scenario planning in this light, as is illustrated by his take on this:

> "Scenarios are stories. They are works of art, rather than scientific analyses. Maybe the reliability of their content is less important than the types of conversations and decisions they spark ."

Scenarios in two steps

Writing relevant and inspiring future scenarios is a craft in itself. If you have ever taken part in a scenario planning project, you may have witnessed that one team member relished to draft scenario stories whereas another team member found it difficult and frustrating. Good scenarios share certain features. To start with, they need to have a clear logic to them. By means of an easily understandable chronology (A lead to B, lead to C, etc.) the reader is guided towards an account of a possible future. Good scenarios inspire as well. The reader needs to be taken on journey to the future, as if he or she is exploring the future through a VR headset. A good scenario also needs to unearth some fundamental challenges for the organization, so readers will be called to action.

Developing good future scenarios always follows a two-step approach. In the first step, you will develop the *content* of the scenarios. Their raw ingredients are derived from the external developments (the 'trend complex') you have identified in previous steps. Those ingredients will be translated into different shapes, directions, and quantities in the different scenarios. Once the content, the building blocks and lines of reasoning for the scenarios, is ready, you start detailing and visualizing the scenarios. This second step is all about the *format*, the visualization, of the scenarios. You can opt for prose, for videos, for a newspaper, or an infographic, for instance. In other words, a scenario can take the shape of a chronology, a 'day in the life' of a customer, a diary of an employee, or a 'state of the union' of a president, for instance, or a combination of various formats.

Content

The scenario framework is the starting point for constructing challenging and inspiring future scenarios. External developments previously identified are used to populate the four scenarios. In doing so, you will have to treat autonomous trends differently from uncertainties. Autonomous trends, which are relatively predictable, will take on a relatively similar shape in all scenarios. Common examples are the composition of a population, size of certain customer segments, etcetera. Uncertainties will take on different appearances in different scenarios. Especially with dependent uncertainties (those with a strong correlation with the key uncertainties) you can vary quite a bit.

Inferring or deducing how dependent developments manifest themselves in different scenarios is a creative process. One in which imagination plays an important role. Team members will need to continually contemplate on how certain impactful developments will unfold given the assumptions of the scenario framework. Sunergie, for instance, had to deduce what kind of distribution structure or types of services would take shape in a market in which online sales would be dominant versus one in which a more traditional market would still be the case. It is important to realize that translating the external developments identified at the previous stage is merely a starting point. Metaphorically, they are the outside pieces of a jigsaw puzzle. The other puzzle pieces needed to craft imaginative scenarios will be generated from other sources, such as the intuition, vision, experience, and logic of the members of the scenario team.

When drafting the scenarios, it is best to work 'outside in' and 'from big to small'. With the final picture (the combination of the two key uncertainties in a specific quadrant) in mind, you will need to string a chain of causes together that will result in that specific final picture. Such a chronology, a 'history of the future' as some scenario planners dub it, will take you on a journey to the situation in the target year of the time horizon. That situation will eventually need to be outlined in a narrative of the world that the organization might find itself in. In such a narrative you will, of course, need to zoom in a bit more on themes and factors relevant for answering the focal question. For instance, what needs will customers have? How about their purchasing power? What will competitors be able to offer? Will there be substitutes for our products or services? Etcetera. Based on some good scenario outlines, the scenario team will ultimately have to formulate the most pressing challenges in every scenario. What are the major issues that the organization will need to frame a response to?

Causes

A proper definition of the whole chain of events that can lead to the final picture in the target year of the scenarios is of great importance. A compelling description of subsequent events or developments will take the reader along on a journey to the future. It will make the scenarios more plausible. In our extensive experience, we have found that when no attention is paid to *how* certain scenarios might come about, they will be deemed less realistic. And when a scenario is not deemed realistic or plausible, it will lose its legitimacy as a foundation for decision-making. People will then ask, you might say the future will look like this, but on what grounds? There's no magic formula for developing a good chronology. It often proves helpful - using the trend complex- to reason which events would have occurred in order to result in the final picture. Some scenario planners will use *reverse engineering*. With the picture of the future as a starting point, they reason back to the here and now step by step. We invite you to experiment and discover what works for you.

Don't forget important events and stakeholders

When writing a chronology ensure that you at least include the most important events, and preferably the behavior of important actors (stakeholders), as well. A scenario can quickly lose credibility when a deciding factor or interest is left out of the equation.

A helpful tool to make a chronology come to life is to develop a timeline. Figure 19 presents possible events that can lead to Sunergie's first scenario.

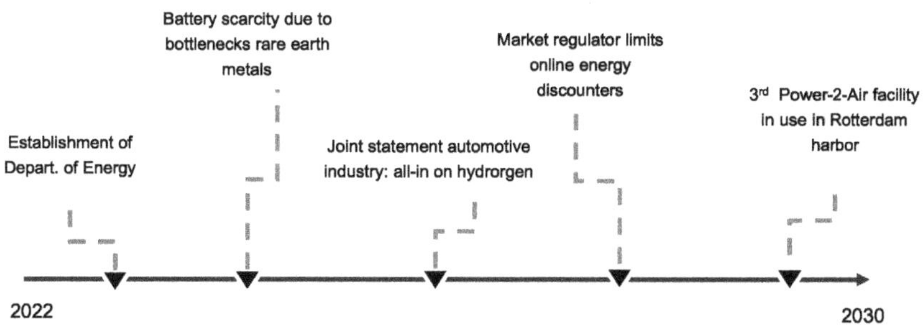

Figure 19: timeline of scenario 1 for Sunergie

Description of the situation

Every scenario should contain a good description of the situation. This is a unique description of the business environment of the organization in the chosen target year. In order to develop a good description, the direct environment of the organization is a good starting point. Porter's 5-forces model provides a helpful structure for this. You can paint a fairly detailed picture of the direct environment by describing – for every scenario- how customers and competitors will behave, whether there are substitutes or new entrants, and how suppliers position themselves.

When you detail the situational description, it is important to refer back to the scope. The picture of the future you want to paint needs to include enough information and detail in order to answer the focal and subquestions. Does it 'check all the boxes'?

Challenges

By using a coherent chronology and a clear and illustrative situational description, a scenario will guide the reader towards inferring logical implications of that scenario. Every scenario will present certain challenges for the organization. Challenges can refer to issues such as shortages, bottlenecks, market demand, competitive behaviors and dynamics, changes in legislation or regulation, etcetera. It is important to concisely describe the most fundamental challenges in each scenario, as these challenges can be used as a focal point for the imagination and creativity of the readers. Relevant and intriguing challenges will instantly switch their brains into solution-finding mode.

Format

The content of a scenario consists of a chronology, a situational description, and a set of fundamental challenges. This content will decide whether a scenario will be deemed relevant, plausible, divergent, and challenging. However, strong content does not necessarily make a scenario memorable. This is where the format comes into play. The age-old adage of 'a picture paints a thousand words' certainly applies to scenarios as well.

Fortunately, there are many ways in which you can bring the content of scenarios to life and trigger an emotional response with the readers/users. A good starting point for appealing to their imagination is by labeling each scenario. A catchy title of a scenario, which also captures its essence, will ensure that that scenario will be more easily understood and remembered. When developing labels, it is crucial that they inspire creativity and imagination yet in such a way that everybody more or less has the same connotations. Sunergie chose the following labels (see figure 18).

- **Local Supplier**: in this first scenario local installers remain the dominant channel for solar panels.
- **Online Outlet**: in this second scenario consumers will bargain hunt online for solar panels.
- **Services Nearby**: in this third scenario local installers need to offer consumers a suite of complex service, a package deal of solar panels, home batteries, and maintenance, for instance.
- **Online Solutions**: in the fourth scenario, complex services and all-in solutions will be offered predominantly online.

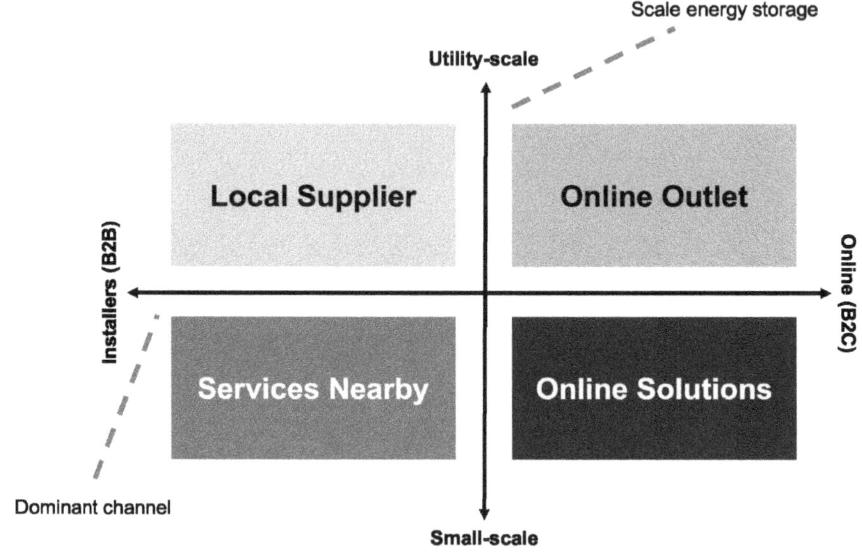

Figure 20: scenarios for Sunergie

Using labels will set the readers off on the right track but the form of the scenarios will determine how well they can identify with and/or imagine a scenario. There are many ways to visualize scenarios, ranging from outcome reports to videos or interactive websites. In this book, we want to introduce you to four commonly used forms of visualization you (and your team) can develop rapidly and easily. Each of the four scenarios for Sunergie serves as an illustration of one of the four formats: a factual description, newspaper headlines, an infographic, and a 'day in the life' narrative. Please browse through these examples and discover which one appeals to you most. Of course, you can always use multiple formats for a scenario so they reinforce one another.

Scenarios as factual descriptions

A factual description is the most commonly used format. It details a scenario with a matter-of-fact narrative. Much attention is paid to the chronology and the characteristics of the future. A big advantage of this format is that the reader is really pulled into the scenario and its logic, thereby making it easier for her or him to accept the scenario as a foundation for decision-making.

> ### Scenario 1: Local Supplier, in factual description format
>
> **Large scale sustainability**
>
> It is 2030. The energy transition is in full swing. Across the globe, a political consensus between the left and right has been formed around the notion that time is of the essence and urgent action needs to be taken, as exemplified by the 2025 Paris Agreement 2.0. In Europe, 'Brussels' and national governments alike have taken the reigns of the energy transition with vigor. Their ambitions are sky-high. Governments, such as the Dutch government in the Hague, favor large-scale renewable initiatives, as progress needs to be made rapidly. In order to finance their grand energy masterplans, subsidies for individual consumers of solar panels, home batteries, and heat pump systems have been scaled down. Large energy companies have altered course. After the 'green shareholder coup' of 2024, Shell has gone all in on wind and solar parks as well as hydrogen. Other energy giants have invested in large-scale energy storage mediums, such as power-to-air. Additionally, locally generated electricity is traded and stored on a massive scale. When the sun goes down, the stored energy is converted back to electricity and sold back to consumers. The Netherlands has not been able to wean itself off gas. Rather, a

different kind of gas now flows through the gas grids. Entire neighborhoods are being converted from natural gas to hydrogen for home heating and cooking tops. Gas grid operators have been successful in persuading the government not to write off the gas grid but to repurpose it for a more sustainable gas.

Consumers only invest in generation

The consumer's need for home batteries has taken a drastic hit. Solar panels, however, are still as popular as ever, as energy you do not use directly is sold off and then stored at utility-scale. The energy landscape that has taken shape over the years has become rather complex. There are many rules and regulations that energy solutions in homes need to adhere to. This also applies to those who install these. Consumers therefore favor trusted, reliable parties with track records. They especially trust certified installers. Consumers have become wary of online discounters or moonlighters and prefer to be informed by trusted and qualified parties regarding what would be the most efficient and affordable options for their specific household's situation. The consumer does not want to browse endless websites of online suppliers. They desire full-service solutions, even if it comes at a price. Costs are not irrelevant but certainly not the most deciding factor. The high complexity of the market and the amount of regulation has made the energy market not that appealing to new entrants and has also stimulated a higher degree of specialization in the value chain.

Scenarios as headlines

Another powerful format for presenting scenarios is to visualize them as newspaper headlines or -in video format- as a news broadcast. This enables you to communicate both causes and characteristics in a way that really captures the 'zeitgeist' of a scenario. The added benefit of this format is that developing it is a fun and engaging exercise for the scenario team.

Figure 21: scenario 2: Online Outlet, as headlines

Scenarios as infographic

An infographic is a great medium to concisely express and visualize the main characteristics of a scenario. It captures the essence of a scenario in one simple overview. An additional benefit of using infographics, especially if you use a consistent format, is that it can help readers to quickly compare the scenarios. The downside of infographics is that readers are not really familiarized with the scenario logic and narrative. This can make it difficult for readers to accept the validity and plausibility of the scenario first time around. Therefore, we recommend using infographics mostly as an add-on to scenario narratives/factual descriptions and not as stand-alone products.

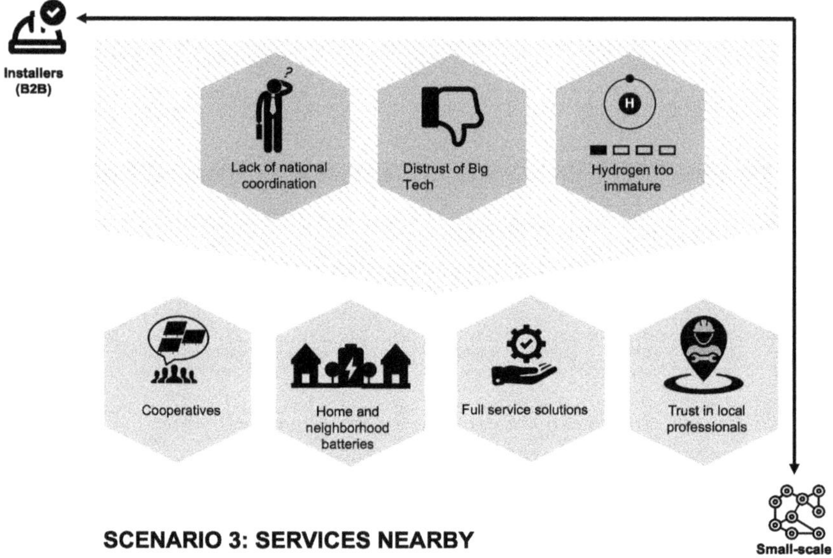

Figure 22: scenario 3: Services Nearby, as infographic

Scenarios as a 'day in the life…' narrative

A great way to illustrate the impact of a scenario on daily life is to use a 'day in the life' or diary format. This can be especially helpful in aiding the reader to think about the implications of a scenario and about possible strategic options or ideas to address those implications.

Scenario 4: Online Solutions- 'day in the life' format

Jane's Monday

Jane wakes up. She takes a glance at her smart phone. March 25th 2030 6:45 am. Time for a quick shower before dropping off the kids at school. She opens her house's energy management app, a force of habit by now. The home battery still has quite some

---

charge to it after all that sunshine yesterday. Should be more than enough for her and her kids' showers. She is really pleased with the smart system the battery is a part of. What a change compared to years ago, when she, as well as a lot of her compatriots, was desperate for alternatives to natural gas as Russia and Middle Eastern suppliers tightened the supply to Europe. Her energy bill went through the roof. The national government was of no assistance back then. Parliament was divided and never able to rally around stable policies. They offered no longer term vision or workable solutions, except for the 'warm sweater weekends' in which gas and electricity were rationed. In face of government inaction, she and Robert - her husband – resigned to searching solutions themselves, like so many others. Their roof was suitable for solar panels and she had seen many ads for home batteries. Through an online price comparison platform she received a great deal on a Solar Home bundle. Solar panels, home batteries, smart appliances, an AI-powered energy trading platform... All part of a fixed monthly cost bundle, just a mouse-click away. And installed the next week! She had also looked at the website of a local installer. However, using them and their partners looked like so much hassle that she quickly lost interest. Through social media Samsung also advertised their complete 'energy ecosystem' but that one turned out to be quite pricey when compared to other providers. Jane is happy with the choice she made. She knows exactly what she gets, the pricing is fair, and the online support is excellent when she needs some assistance. Enough retrospection, she thinks to herself, time for a hot shower.

The scenario workshop

By now, you have a scenario framework, based on two key uncertainties. You probably also have a preference for what you would like the scenarios to look like, what their format(s) should be. But first it is time to generate the actual content of the scenarios. You and your team will do this in a scenario workshop. Once again, you will find out that you can cover quite some ground in only a three-hour session. Especially, if you have a good division of labor within the team.

Preparations

The scenario workshop is a creative workshop. One thing to consider is to invite an external visionary or lateral thinker. Such people can guard the team against tunnel vision or drawing incorrect or too hasty conclusions. Once again, a few helpful templates will go a long way in facilitating the session as well as capturing the insights of the team.

The workshop

After a good preparation, it is time to gather the team once again. The workshop will consist of two parts. Firstly, generating the ingredients for the scenarios and, secondly, using those to construct a short narrative.

For generating the ingredients, we have developed a format for capturing the causes and characteristics for the four scenarios (see figure 23 for the example of Sunergie using this format). As per what might be a bit of a routine by now, you will capture ingredients for the various scenarios on post-its and group them together on the format. You will notice that this will become easier after one or two scenarios, especially as some scenarios are the mirror opposite of one another. Please see figure 23 for Sunergie's example.

During the second part of the workshop, you will use the ingredients you generated in developing mini scenario narratives, or 'scenario outlines.' You will discover that in creating the narratives, you might have to revisit an idea or two. This will only make the scenarios more plausible and relevant. Once you have developed the mini narratives of the four scenarios, take some time to check them for the four criteria of quality frameworks and scenarios. Are all four scenarios plausible, relevant, divergent, and challenging (see Chapter 8)? If this is the case, then you will have laid the groundwork for detailing and visualizing the scenarios (in the formats you desire). A good way to test the narratives is to see if those who have worked on a specific scenario can present a short elevator pitch on that scenario. Is their narrative convincing?

Rip it up!

A 'tear-out' session is a great intermezzo for stimulating creativity during the scenario workshop. In this session, the team will have to peruse numerous magazines and tear out pictures, ads, headlines, etc. and match them to the scenario they think these illustrate best. The tear-out session often leads to new insights and has the added benefit that it forces the team to look for indicators or signposts of the scenarios in current events. This will familiarize the team even more with the scenarios as well as with how those scenarios might come about.

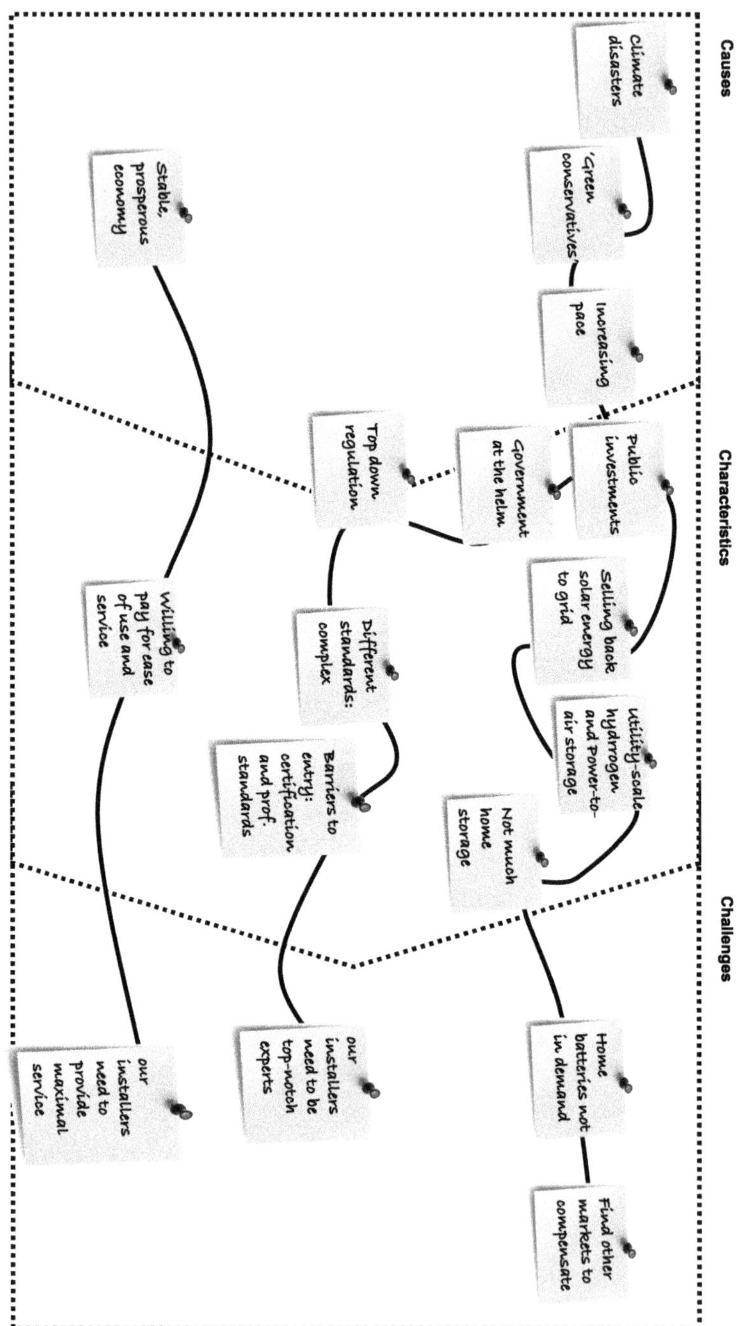

Figure 23: results of Sunergie's brainstorm on causes and characteristics for scenario 1

Golden rules

1. **Adhere to the scope**. Some teams can lose themselves in the creative process of writing scenarios. Creativity is always a good thing. However, ensure that all that creative energy is channeled. Always refer to the scope to see to it that the scenarios deal with the relevant themes and issues for the organization.

2. **Ensure divergence**. Scenarios need to take their readers on a journey to future worlds so they can evaluate choices in the here and now. When making scenarios, accentuate the differences between scenarios, not their similarities. This will ensure that scenarios help you to look at things from different perspectives.

3. **Do not incorporate answers or strategic options in scenario narratives**. Scenarios paint pictures of the *external* business environment and, in doing so, enable organizations to identify challenges and opportunities. It is important not to mix the organization's response to such challenges in the scenario narratives themselves. If responses are part of the scenario narratives, people will often prefer one scenario over another based on the popularity of those responses (wishful thinking). E.g., if somebody reads that their department has been discontinued by the company in a particular scenario, then their dislike for this strategic option will make them not want to consider this scenario. They will (often unconsciously) confuse the desirability with the plausibility of scenarios. Therefore, always try to keep a strict separation between the scenarios themselves -what the external environment demands of the organization- and strategic options flowing from them, the possible responses of the organization to such demands.

10

Step 5: Apply scenarios

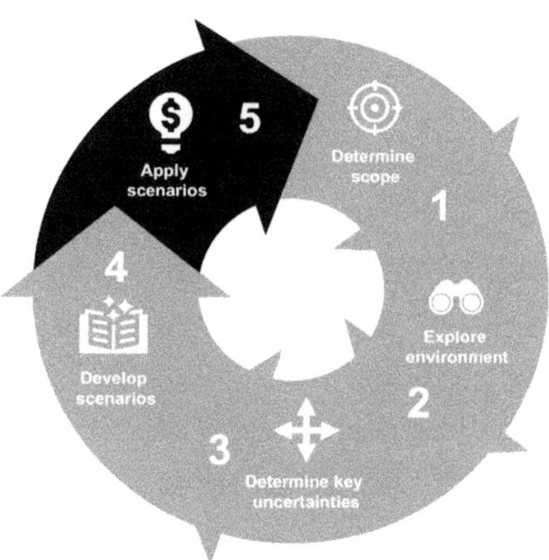

By now the scenarios have been developed. You are ready to use and apply them. If you think that you can now select one preferred scenario, you are, unfortunately, mistaken. Choosing one scenario means speculating on only one possible future, a risky venture for even the most (capital) plush organizations. Instead of selecting one scenario, you will use all of them to arrive at more carefully considered and future-proof choices. In practice, scenarios are extremely helpful to organizations for two main purposes. The first is to generate new ideas. The second is to stress-test the robustness of current plans.

When you use scenarios to generate *new ideas*, whether it is for identifying opportunities for new innovations or for generating strategic options for the direction of your company, the scenarios function as a catalyst. The four extreme yet plausible imaginations of the future, all with their own challenges, will offer an inspiring basis for exploring new opportunities for the organization. More often than not, we find that scenarios initially deemed the most uncomfortable and challenging, ultimately prove to produce the best ideas. Some organizations mainly use scenarios to identify new strategic options and to direct innovation. Often, these companies have a hefty risk appetite, favoring the prospects of bigger returns.

When scenarios are used to *stress-test plans*, be they strategic choices or planned investments, the scenarios function as a framework for evaluation. Plans that have a positive result in all scenarios can be characterized as robust or futureproof. Plans that do not match with every scenario can be adjusted to create a better fit to the scenarios or – if that is not possible- be reconsidered. For some organizations, it is important to be well-prepared for every scenario given their risk appetite or mission statement. Such organizations do not wish to be exposed to much risk and, in turn, are satisfied with stable yet modest returns instead. Other organizations can afford taking more risks, consciously speculating on some scenarios to generate above average returns.

Applying scenarios in three steps

You choose how to apply the scenarios based on the goal of your project. The range of applications varies from learning and inspiring, to testing concrete investment proposals. Frequently, organizations opt for multiple goals. In practice, the following three steps are often chosen: 1. generating strategic options, 2. testing those options, and, finally, 3. making choices. We will tell you a bit more about these three steps below.

1.Generating strategic options

Good scenarios are extreme yet plausible and always relevant to some of the biggest strategic questions for the organization. By exploring futures that can be each other's opposite/mirror image, they cover much of the ground along which the future might unfold. Every scenario has certain implications relating to the focal question of the organization. A scenario's implications are a call to action. They can be framed as opportunities, concrete challenges, bottlenecks, shortages, latent/future consumer needs, etcetera. In Sunergie's first scenario, for instance, there are challenges related to a disappointing demand for home batteries. In that scenario – as well as another one- large-scale, centralized energy storage solutions are dominant, diminishing the need for decentralized energy storage solutions. The first scenario also presents Sunergie with challenges regarding its distribution, as stringent regulations and certifi-cations demand the highest degree of expertise and craftsmanship of installers.

The implications of the scenarios always demand responses. These are often formulated as strategic options for the organization. Figure 24 illustrates how challenges invite reactions, bottlenecks can demand solu-tions or workarounds, shortages can require new resources or suppliers, and changes in consumer demand can trigger new products or services. There is no set-in-stone or single best format for generating strategic options. Sometimes they are so obvious that they automatically flow from a well-formulated implication. A brainstorm with experts can sometimes also help a scenario team to create valid and solid options.

This is exactly what happened at Sunergie. The scenario team recruited a select few other colleagues with whom they would discuss the biggest challenges in the scenarios and generate strategic options. In scenario 1, they identified concrete options such as selling the exclusive import rights for their home battery business, but also focusing on more exclusive partnerships with selected installation companies, or even creating their own certification program for distribution and installation partners.

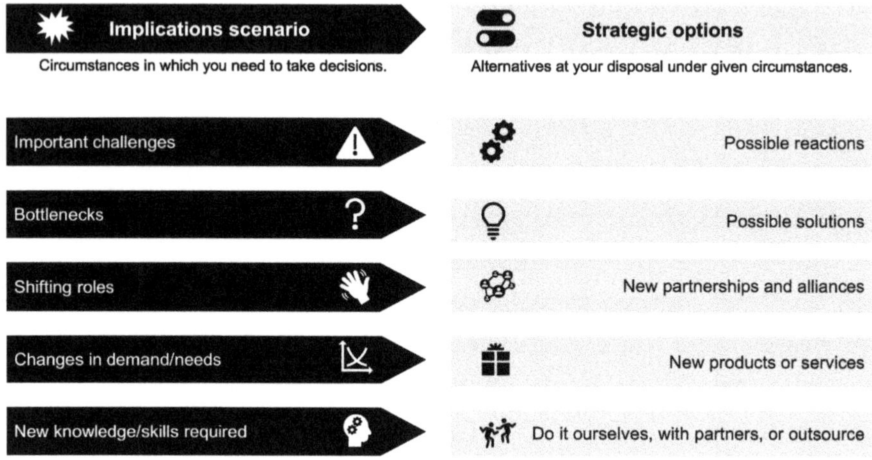

Figure 24: implications and strategic options

2. Testing strategic options

Scenarios are not only great catalysts for strategic options but provide a good framework to test those options as well. Scenarios will be helpful at (stress-)testing the robustness of both new strategic options and current strategic plans alike. When a new option or a component of the current strategy is relevant in every scenario, it can be considered robust. When that option or choice does not match adequately with one or more scenarios, then that option can be deemed risky.

Sometimes organizations start with testing their current strategy before identifying new strategic options. We often refer to testing the current strategy as 'wind tunnelling'. Just as with testing the aerodynamics of, for instance, an airplane, the organization's strategy will be placed in a wind tunnel. In this case, the four scenarios will constitute the metaphorical wind tunnel. Which elements will hold, which elements will fly off? In order to properly relate the strategy to the scenarios, it is important to first dissect the strategy. Sunergie's strategy consisted of, amongst others, supplying both solar panels and home batteries to installers. These elements of the strategy can therefore be dissected into three items Sunergie can test in the scenarios:

1. Product range: solar panels
2. Product range: home batteries
3. Sale channel: installers

You can use a *scenario/option matrix* for assessing the fit of the strategic choices with the four scenarios. Table 8 shows the matrix for Sunergie. The black diamonds illustrate the match of a strategic choice with an individual scenario. By totalling the black diamonds in each row, you generate a score for how well a choice fits with the external environment; in this case, the four scenarios. The higher the score, the bigger the match and the smaller the risk involved. Conversely, the lower the score, the smaller the fit with the external environment and bigger the risk of that choice.

	Local Supplier	Online Outlet	Services Nearby	Online Solutions	Total
Home batteries	◆◇◇	◇◇◇	◆◆◆	◆◆◇	6
Solar panels	◆◆◆	◆◆◆	◆◆◆	◆◆◆	12
Installers	◆◆◇	◇◇◇	◆◆◆	◆◇◇	6
Online shop	◆◇◇	◆◆◆	◆◇◇	◆◆◆	8

Table 8: scenario/option matrix for Sunergie's strategic choices

When looking at Sunergie's matrix, you can conclude that it should focus more on solar panels. As solar panels have a great fit with every scenario they are a 'no regret' option. Home batteries, however, only match with half of them. Home batteries therefore are 'scenario specific' or a 'big bet', something Sunergie might want to reconsider. Also, relying exclusively on installers as a sales channel is risky in several scenarios. Setting up an online shop, however, might prove to be relevant in most scenarios, or at least not detrimental. This is what scenario planners call a 'safety net' option: an option with relatively limited investments involved, which can be scaled up or down easily when conditions change. In other words, not the best, not the worst fit, but their low costs and scalability make them worth considering.

3. Making choices

With 'wind tunnelling' one can assess the risk profile of an organization's current strategy. Is the strategy relevant in multiple futures? Wind tunnelling can also be used to assess how new strategic options stack up against multiple scenarios. Once you have done that, you can use that information to make concrete choices. Does it make sense to stop with certain past choices? Maybe it is time to invest in new strategic options that fit with scenarios the current strategy is ill-prepared for?

Scenario planning will help with laying the proper foundation for such choices. However, you first need to decide what your risk appetite is. Do you only want to choose options that are 'no regret', which match with every scenario? If that is the case, you are not willing to take much risk. Perhaps you want your choices to optimally position your organization for one specific scenario. In that case, you have a high risk appetite. If that scenario will ultimately manifest, you will profit greatly. If not, well, you better have thought of some mitigation measures. Schnaars (1986) has categorized four risk variants that you can use to inform your choices. He discerns a robust, a flexible, a multiple, and a gamble/

'bet the farm' strategy (see figure 25). It is helpful to give some good thoughts to which variants suit you and/or your organization.

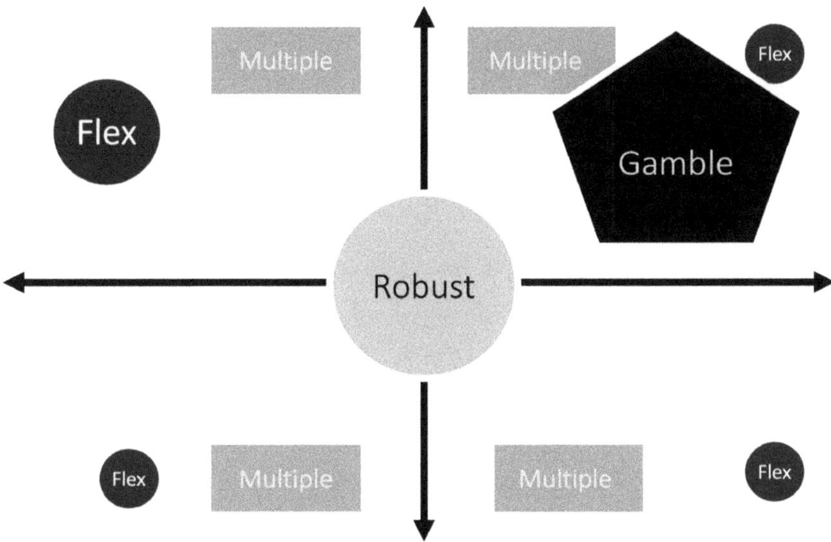

Figure 25: risk variants for strategic choices

Robust strategy

If you opt for the robust strategy, you have a small risk appetite and will usually choose strategic options or make strategic choices that will perform well in every scenario. Given their mission, this is an often-favored strategy of public organizations. For businesses, such a robust strategy will offer only a limited (yet stable) profit but will also prevent large strategic failures. In Sunergie's current strategy there are a few robust elements. Especially the focus on solar panels remains beyond doubt and will prove to be a robust, important element in Sunergie's strategy.

It is, however, not said that risk-averse organizations do not make very targeted choices as a result of a scenario exercise. Sometimes wind tunneling the existing strategy leads to the realization that the organization has a blind spot in light of a particular scenario. Therefore, maximum effort must be made on that specific scenario in order to arrive at a robust strategy overall.

Flexible strategy

If you choose a flexible strategy, you keep your options open as long as possible by investing in all scenarios while retaining the possibility to scale up or down. Especially in operating environments with a lot of change and uncertainty, a flexible strategy is a common one. Choosing a flexible strategy will mean that you will need to monitor your external environment closely and frequently. When this environment changes, and a specific scenario is becoming increasingly likely, you need to be able to act decisively. In the next chapter you can read more about monitoring the external environment. Following internal discussions, Sunergie opted for setting up their own online shop. This initiative is especially relevant in scenarios where the current sales channel (installers) loses its value. Sunergie's management team also saw a lot of potential in being able to quickly scale up this strategic option if necessary. A variant of this strategy is a 'core-satellite' strategy. This is a strategy in which an organization chooses to focus a bit more on one scenario. For instance, the one deemed most likely. However, it also invests in options that fit with other scenarios; a 40-20-20-20% division, for example.

Multiple strategy

Perhaps you are a portfolio manager at a large private equity firm or multinational. For large, cash rich organizations a multiple strategy is feasible. It comes down to being able to make considerable investments in all four scenarios. Some of these will flourish. Others you might need to write off or depreciate more quickly than anticipated. A multiple strategy is all about maximal diversification, limiting its risks.

Gamble strategy

With this strategy you put all of your eggs in one basket. You deliberately decide to choose options matching with only one or two scenarios, realizing and accepting (!) that this presents considerable risks if other scenarios were to ultimately materialize.

Strategy risks

Most organizations use scenarios to generate new strategic options or stress-test their strategy. Some also use scenarios as a risk management tool. With risk management, most focus is often placed on operational risks. In other words, risks that can hamper the *execution* of the strategy. With scenario planning you can also identify strategy risks. These are risks that endanger the *validity* of the strategy. In each scenario you can explore which specific strategy risks might arise. For instance, new regulations, a competitor's new factory, or vertical integration by a supplier. Just like with wind tunneling new strategic options, you can test how these strategy risks stack up against all scenarios. If a particular strategy risk is plausible and rather likely in every scenario, this one should receive your full attention. You will need to formulate a strategic response to that one. For strategy risks that only manifest themselves in a few scenarios, monitoring them will often suffice.

The scenario application workshop

Using four inspiring scenarios to work towards concrete results is always a lot of fun. Perhaps you share the experience that working on making strategic choices can be an arduous process. Consensus is often hard to arrive at, as participants have different (fundamental) assumptions regarding what the future will look like. The advantage of scenario planning is that you embrace and acknowledge the validity of those different opinions. One team member might think one specific scenario is the most likely, another might choose a different scenario. As long as the set of scenarios is regarded as relevant and plausible, it is possible to collectively work towards making robust strategic choices. Discussing the future and strategic options at your disposal, the *strategic conversation*, can be organized within a three-hour session.

Preparations

A *scenario game* is a fun yet meaningful activity to kick off such a session with. If needed, you can even do this with a large group. The purpose of the game is to learn more about the four scenarios and especially how everyone relates to them in their own way. In this game you literally ask participants to take a position on the scenario framework.

You prepare this portion of the session by drawing a scenario framework on the room's floor. You can do this with masking tape. In each quadrant of the framework, you can place an infographic with the most important traits of that scenario, for instance. You can use easels for this, or tape them to a flip chart. Before playing the game, four people will each need to 'pitch' a scenario.

The workshop

After a short introduction and the scenario pitches, you will start the game. Participants are invited to 'vote with their feet'. A facilitator will first need to ask participants to walk to the center of the scenario framework. In the first round of the game, the participants are asked to walk over to the quadrant, the scenario, they think is most like the world we live in today. In the second round, they need to walk to the scenario they think is most likely/probable. In the third round they can be asked to go to the scenario they think is most challenging, or the organization is least prepared for. All the while, the facilitator will ask people to explain why they chose to go to a specific scenario. This is not only a great way to experience the scenarios together but especially to learn from each other. Learning about why somebody regards one scenario to be more probable than others, for instance, can teach people about what (other) signals for the future people pick up on and how they interpret them. Perhaps during this session, a consensus emerges regarding which scenario is deemed most likely. If that scenario is also considered the most challenging one, well, then the organization knows rather quickly where to focus its efforts on!

After the scenario game, subgroups will brainstorm on strategic options with which to respond to the most important challenges of a specific scenario. It is important to ensure that the strategic options are relevant for that specific scenario. Depending on the time available, you can let every group rotate in order to cover all four scenarios, taking less time per scenario as previous groups have already given input. For instance, group 1 starts with scenario 1 and then moves on to 2, 3, and 4; group 2 starts with scenario 2, then moves on to 3, 4, and 1, etc. If time is scarce, you can also let each group cover only two diagonally opposed scenarios, forcing them to think about two completely different futures. We have developed a template with which you can capture the strategic options (see figure 26). Once you have covered all four scenarios, you can discuss how well the identified options match with all four scenarios. Doing so, will give you insights into which options are robust and which ones are riskier. You can let groups select a top-3 of options per scenario, for time management purposes. The results of the scenario game can also come in handy once the fit of the options with the scenarios is determined. Options with the best fit to the scenarios deemed most likely and/or challenging are often ones that need to be prioritized for detailing at a later time.

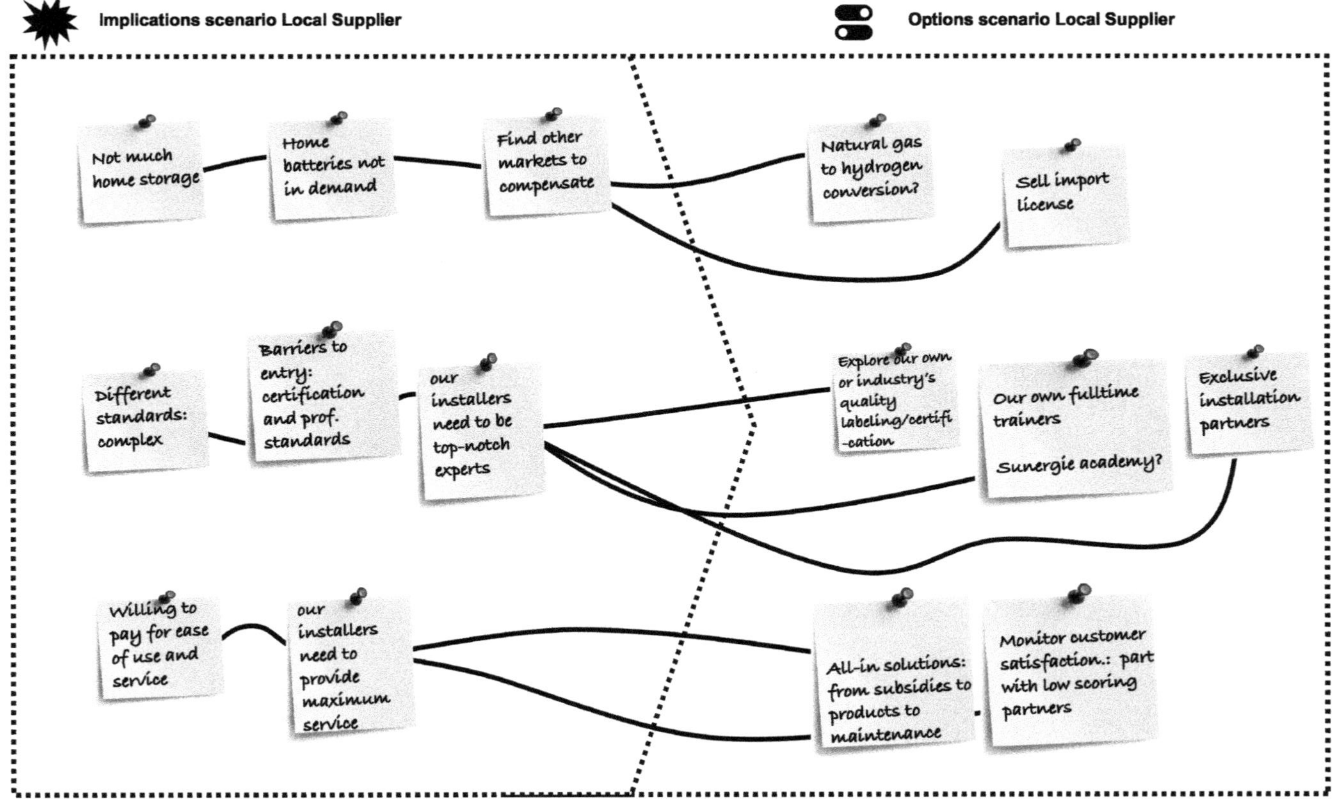

Figure 26: results of Sunergie's brainstorm on strategic options for one scenario

Golden rules

1. **Focus on the most important challenges**. When brainstorming for strategic options, it is important to limit yourself to a select number of challenges related to the most pressing and vitally important implications of a scenario. The more focus, the more concrete and actionable the options will be.

2. **Try to make options more robust.** If one scenario has inspired you to generate an innovative, new strategic option, you can use the other scenarios to make that option more robust. Sometimes a few tweaks (for instance, regarding timing, scale, or choice of partners) can really make a difference to how robust and future-proof a strategic option can be.

3. **Take calculated risks**. Risks are inherent to making choices. We do not advocate using scenarios as a tool to avoid taking risks; use them for taking calculated risks and thinking about mitigating those risks. For instance, if you choose options that fit one or two scenarios, you can already think about ways how to make them flexible enough to scale them up or down if changes in the external environment demand so.

11

Monitor and adapt with scenarios

In the previous chapters you have reviewed the five steps of scenario planning. Perhaps you already made same liner notes and thought about uncertainties, scenarios, or strategic options for your organization, or, who knows, perhaps even for your personal life. Maybe you already set things in motion for starting a scenario project with the aim of stress-testing your own organization's strategy. We think that is great, but before you do so, we ask you to read this chapter before you spring into action. With this chapter we want to show you that using scenarios once can be very helpful and inspiring, yet you will get most out of scenario planning if you use it as a structural, and imbedded, method to monitor change in your external environment. It helps to keep this in mind before you start your scenario project.

Well-thought-out scenarios are not only a powerful tool to arrive at future-proof choices and decisions, but also to continue monitoring your external environment. It, regrettably, is not uncommon for scenario teams to put a lot of effort into developing scenarios, helping decision makers to carefully consider strategic choices and plans, yet for the scenarios to end up in a proverbial drawer once that has all been done. A pity, we believe, as those same scenarios that have been used to identify strategic options and stress-test strategic choices can form a great framework to monitor change in the external environment. You can regard a set of four scenarios as a photograph recording the uncertainty in an organization's external environment at a given time. Every scenario is roughly equally relevant and probable. By using a set of scenarios to monitor change, you can turn that picture into a film, a motion picture. Over time, you will notice how certain scenarios are becoming increasingly likely, while others decrease in likelihood. This has implications for which strategic options or possible choices will become more relevant, which investments need to be scaled up and, conversely, which ones need to be scaled down. Scenarios therefore enable you to adapt to a changing external environment.

Some organizations therefore use scenarios to structurally monitor their external operating environment and adapt their strategic course accordingly. We know of some excellent examples. Yet, many organizations find this difficult to do. Sometimes they seem to be trapped in a hard to break cycle in which a new strategy is made every three or four years. Sometimes the planning and control cycle is organized so rigidly around a good implementation of the strategy that making changes midway is difficult and deemed outright undesirable. Sometimes the financial results are deemed so sound that no sense of urgency is felt to really consider how the organization can continue to add value in a changing environment. However understandable these reasons are, they are no excuse not to look at the validity of your strategy more often. Only when you are able to frequently recalibrate to your changing external environment and use those insights to adapt your choices and plans, can you truly be a learning organization.

The early warning system (EWS)

Let us suppose you want to be a learning organization. In that case you will want to set up an early warning system (EWS) in which you can use the scenarios as lenses with which to recognize and interpret (nascent) signals of change in your external environment. If you have practiced developing scenarios, you will already have a feel for this. Because you have thought about various extremely different futures you will probably see signposts of change all around you. You will read the paper or watch the news differently. You probably will see signals hinting at one or more scenarios everywhere. This enables you to contemplate their implications more rapidly and to decrease your time to react to them.

Change indicators (signposts)

Some organizations working with scenarios only use them on an ad hoc, impromptu, basis. Once every while they think about the likelihood of the scenarios they developed. Other organizations develop a structured early warning system that is based on the key uncertainties that underpin their scenario framework. The first step in designing an EWS is always to consider which factors can inform the likelihood of the scenarios and therefore need to be monitored. Since the key uncertainties shaping the scenarios will by and large define the shape of the organization's future operating environment, it is important to list change indicators that are indicative of these uncertainties.

Let us once again turn to the example of Sunergie. One of their key uncertainties is the scale on which energy will be stored. Will large, utility scale energy storage be dominant? Or decentralized, small-scale solutions, such as home batteries? You can think of change indicators for both ends of that axis of the framework. For instance, government regulations or technological breakthroughs can result in energy to be stored in large-scale solutions. Whereas an increase in local government subsidies for homeowners, an increase of the number of home battery manufacturers, or the establishment of local energy companies or co-operatives all can hint at decentralization.

Assessing such change indicators can be a task of the scenario team, but you can also establish an expert panel to this end. Organizations that frequently and structurally monitor their external environment for change often make use of a panel consisting of both internal and external experts. Doing this enables them to make carefully considered appraisals of the occurrence of change indicators and has the added benefit of comparing both internal and external points of view. Involving external experts or stakeholders is extremely valuable in assessing whether tunnel vision is present internally. Such tunnel vision inhibits objective assessment of changes in the external environment. Comparing internal and external indicator assessments is also helpful in establishing whether the organization has adequate information regarding certain change indicators. Discussing internal and external differences can trigger interesting discussions whether an organization has access to the same or accurate information as the external panel members or whether there is some information asymmetry that needs to be addressed. Equally interesting, if internal and external experts use the same information, how can it be that it is interpreted differently? Having these discussions can unearth interesting insights to take on board for adapting to changes in the external environment.

Dashboarding

Assessing whether the individual likelihood of all the scenarios is in- or decreasing based on a frequent analysis of the change indicators, is the essence of an Early Warning System (EWS). You could argue that when you have just developed a set of scenarios, their probability is roughly equal (25% times 4). This is because you have tried to identify the key uncertainties, the '50/50s' at a given time. However, as time goes by and events and developments occur, scenario probabilities change. After some time, you might find that due to external developments a certain scenario has significantly increased in probability. Conversely, others then will have decreased in likelihood. It goes without saying that strategic options for the most likely scenario need to be implemented or scaled up. Strategic options that fit the lesser likely scenario need to be scaled back.

When you consider using an EWS, it is important to design a good dashboard. Luckily some good online tools are available for this. Just google 'environmental monitor scenarios' or 'early warning system'. Of course, the dashboard needs to illustrate the current likelihood of the scenarios. You want to know the *'leading'* scenario, after all. Knowing how the likelihood has changed over time can also be relevant information. Especially if you can trace this back to certain change indicators.

You get the best value out of such a system if you can relate the dashboard with your organization's strategy. You can tie the most important choices or new strategic options to the four scenarios. A strategic option will become more relevant as the scenarios it has a good match with increase in likelihood. An organization can define a certain threshold value, which, when reached, converts the option into an actual choice or decision. For current plans or choices, it is the other way around. If certain scenarios score below a minimum probability threshold, and therefore also the relevance of a certain choice, then that choice needs to be reconsidered.

Sunergie uses an EWS and has also designed a dashboard. Figure 27 illustrates how the probabilities of the scenarios have changed. The important conclusion after a year is that the expert panel deems small-scale energy storage more likely. Yet in terms of distribution channel, it is still a toss-up, as both the left and right squares are roughly equal in size.

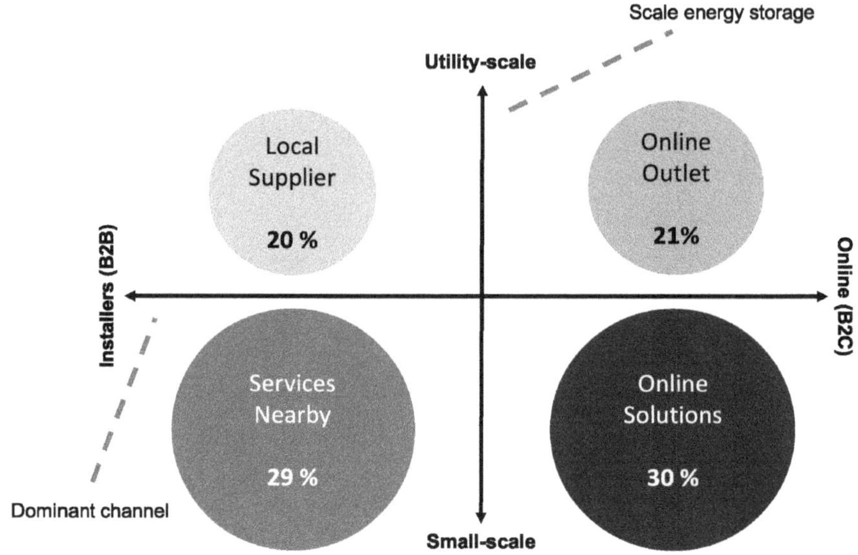

Figure 27: a visual representation of Sunergie's scenarios' probability after one year

Institutionalization

Using an EWS to monitor changes in the external environment and to make sense of the signposts and indicators goes a long way towards becoming a learning organization. If you have followed the steps of developing scenarios this book outlines, then you will have laid a strong foundation for an EWS. The challenge then will not be so much the technical development and deployment of one, but really how to institutionalize it within your organization. In practice, an EWS can often be regarded as a great 'gadget' tied to an individual strategist or risk manager. To prevent the EWS becoming the hobby horse of one individual, organizations are well-advised to embed it in their planning and control cycle. Every autumn, new annual plans are developed for the coming year. Most of the time, the planning and control cycle has an inward-looking orientation: how are we doing regarding the execution of our strategy ('are we *doing things right*')? Commonly, last year's blueprints are recycled after some minor tweaks as directed by the higher-ups.

Insights from an EWS are valuable information to take onboard in a planning and control cycle. The summer, when preparations start for new plans and budgets, can often be a great time to organize a (survey) round for the EWS. These insights, along with internal ones, can inform the plans for next year. Ideally, c-level will interpret the data from the EWS (are we doing the *right things?*) and use those insights to develop instructions that departments or business units will translate into their annual plans. For instance, c-level can decide that some investments need to be scaled up, that new projects need to be initiated, or that certain existing choices need to scale back a bit.

Sunergie has used the scenarios and EWS to review their choices. One of their most important conclusions was to continue importing and selling home batteries. The results from their first EWS round indicated the small-scale storage scenarios were deemed to have increased in probability, increasing the relevance of that choice. The board therefore chose to scale up Sunergie's long-term contracts with home battery producers.

The early warning workshop

Deciding which indicators to monitor lies at the heart of each functional EWS. These indicators are logically coupled to the key uncertainties that form the scenario framework as these key uncertainties set the scenarios in motion. The scenario team can deduce a good set of indicators in a two-hour workshop. If at the onset of a scenario project you already know that you wish to use an EWS, you can work the indicator session into the workshop in which you decide on the key uncertainties or the one in which you identify causes and characteristics of the scenarios.

Preparations

In the early warning workshop, you will look for indicators that can be tied to the key uncertainties. You will monitor these indicators over time. You can monitor by means of an expert panel, or by means of research. More often than you think, longitudinal research is openly available in which some indicators will be reported on throughout many years. In preparation of the workshop, it can help to identify available data sources.

If your key uncertainties are economic in nature, then it might be helpful to look at data of national statistics offices, banks, or industry associations. For political or social indicators national statistics offices or think tanks often have valuable data. Spatial indicators can often be found in data from government (urban and/or spatial) planning offices. You might be pleasantly surprised by the sheer amount of publicly available data of statistics and research offices, as well as other sources.

The workshop

During the workshop you will try to find change indicators for the key uncertainties. There are several ways in which you can do this. In our experience, assigning indicators to the two 'extremes' of the key uncertainties (the pluses and the minuses, so to speak) is a great starting point. This is like looking at four wind directions and translating the interplay of their combined forces into the probability of the scenarios.

When identifying possible change indicators, it is recommended to refer back to the nature of their uncertainty. Is their effect/consequence or their progression uncertain? You can also refer to the scenarios themselves to look at what consequences these uncertainties produce or certain causes. After referring back, you commence brainstorming on the change indicators. The main thing to keep in mind is which events or developments can be indicative for a situation in the future. We have developed a simple format you can use for this exercise. Figure 28 shows the example of Sunergie for some inspiration. Once you have a list of possible indicators, you can make a final selection in which you need to ensure that for each 'extreme' of the axes an equal number of indicators is selected. We use online tooling in which we use the indicators in a survey we send to an expert panel. In the survey, we ask participants to assign a likelihood to the indicator. For instance, 'How likely is it that by 2030 the number of hydrogen plants has doubled?' or 'How likely is it that by 2030 50% of consumers orders their solar panels online'.

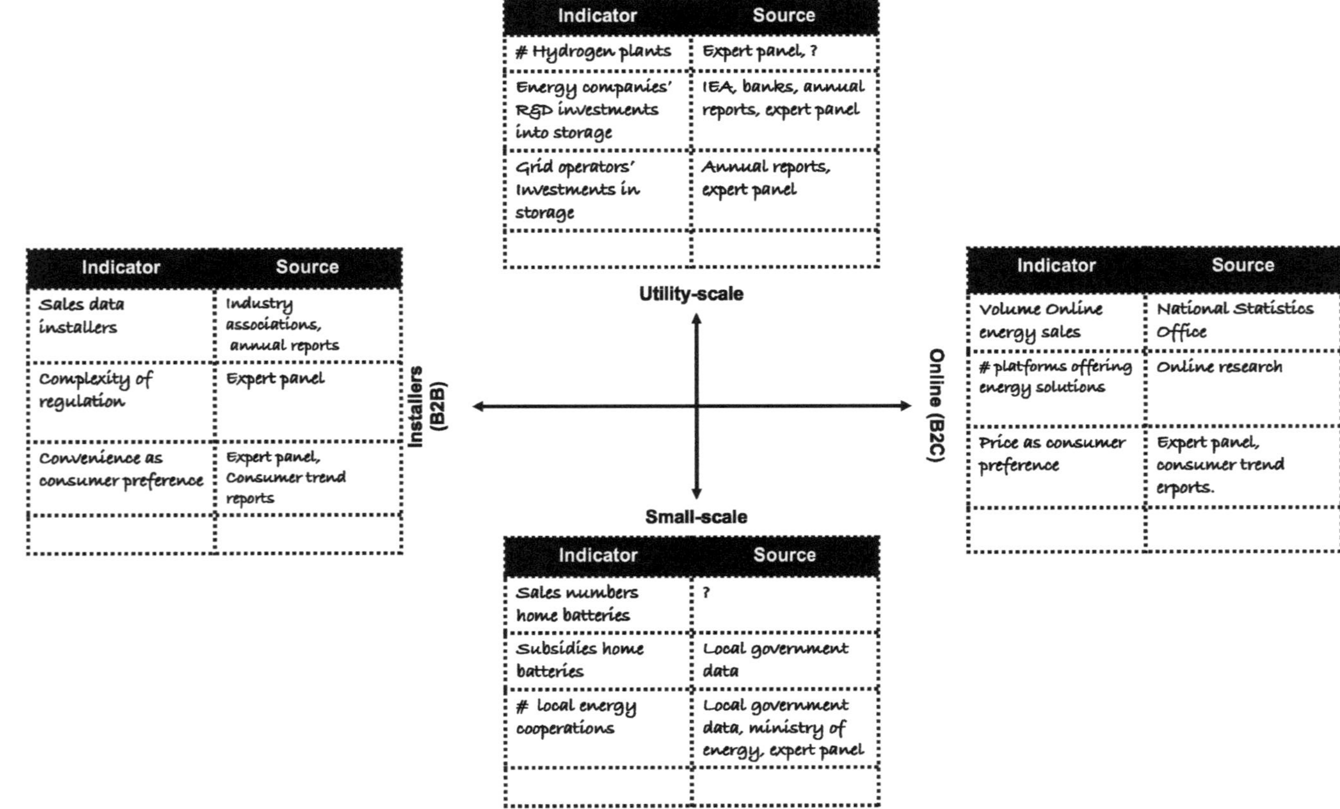

Utility-scale

Indicator	Source
# Hydrogen plants	Expert panel, ?
Energy companies' R&D investments into storage	IEA, banks, annual reports, expert panel
Grid operators' Investments in storage	Annual reports, expert panel

Installers (B2B)

Indicator	Source
Sales data installers	Industry associations, annual reports
Complexity of regulation	Expert panel
Convenience as consumer preference	Expert panel, Consumer trend reports

Online (B2C)

Indicator	Source
Volume Online energy sales	National Statistics Office
# platforms offering energy solutions	Online research
Price as consumer preference	Expert panel, consumer trend erports.

Small-scale

Indicator	Source
Sales numbers home batteries	?
Subsidies home batteries	Local government data
# local energy cooperations	Local government data, ministry of energy, expert panel

Figure 28: change indicators brainstorm Sunergie

Golden rules

1. **Focus on the most important options or choices**. When designing an EWS it is important to focus on the most consequential and important choices or strategic options. The ones that involve the most risk are the ones you want to monitor using scenarios.

2. **Do not get too technical**. An EWS can be a valuable tool but be cautious in its use. This is because the system will involve making assumptions, for instance regarding the relation between key uncertainties and indicators or between scenarios and options/choices. We advise to discuss the outcomes of an EWS round with an expert panel before arriving at conclusions.

3. **Look at obsolescence**. Scenarios do 'age' over time. When scenarios are no longer relevant, they no longer broaden thinking about the future but actually narrow it down. Therefore, you need to validate the scenarios once in a while, to ensure that the key uncertainties still are adequately uncertain and valid; and whether the scenarios are still adequately relevant for the changes and challenges in your external environment. You can think of some threshold % of probability for the scenarios they should not go under. For instance, if two scenarios both score under 10% - meaning two other scenarios total 80% or up, then a certain axis can no longer be deemed uncertain and you need to consider a new scenario framework.

4. **Do not be lulled into a false sense of security by data**. Quantitative data can certainly be useful in monitoring how an indicator progresses. However, they are historic by definition and do not guarantee that the past trend will continue towards the future. A good balance between quantitative data and experts' qualitative assessments (how likely do they deem a certain indicator to be in the year of your scenarios) often produces the best results. There are plenty of examples of markets suddenly crashing after years of growth or of previous in-demand products rapidly becoming obsolete by a nascent technology. Disruptions can occur and are

not always predicted by data, whereas certain experts can prove to be quite visionary on the matter with plausible, qualitative reasoning.

We hope that reading this book has inspired you to give scenario planning a go. As with many things, actually practicing scenario planning is the best way to gain experience and familiarity with the method. To get you going we have developed some simple yet effective downloadable formats, which you can use for the workshops that we have described in this book. If you print those on an A0 sized sheet, these should give participants plenty of space for giving their input.

We are proponents of organizing face-to-face brainstorm sessions with a project team, or even some outside/external experts and stakeholders for even more points of view. However, busy schedules, working across time zones, or faced with lockdowns due to a pandemic, for instance, can throw some spanners in the works... Therefore, having online tools available for supporting a scenario project can be rather valuable. You can use generic online brainstorm tools but there are also tailor-made online tools for scenario planning. We have codeveloped one with Toolsfactory.nl, which has augmented scenario planning projects for nearly a decade now.

Formats

You can download the formats by scanning the QR Code below or you can make your own ones inspired by the formats on the next pages.

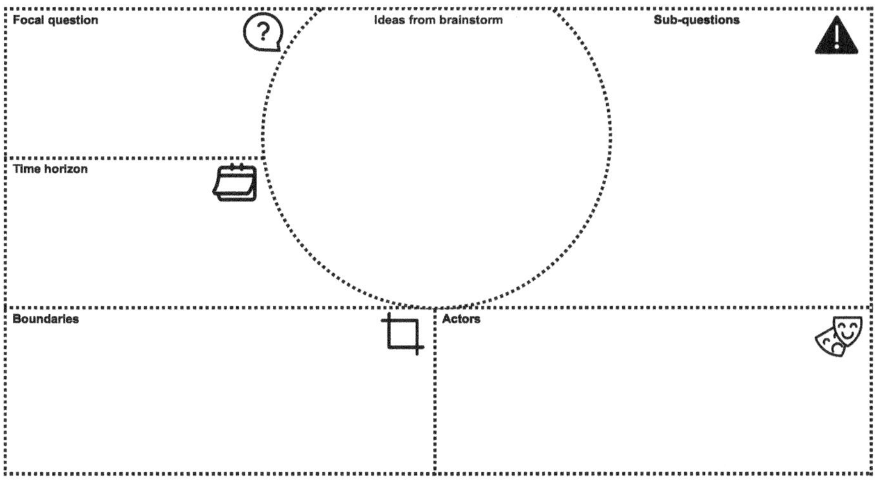

Political	Economic	Social
Technological	Ecological	Demographic

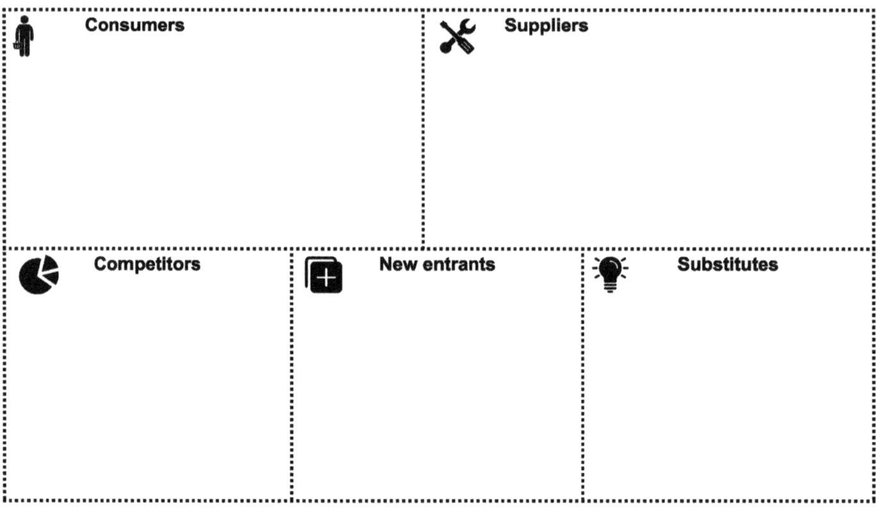
Consumers
Suppliers
Competitors
New entrants
Substitutes

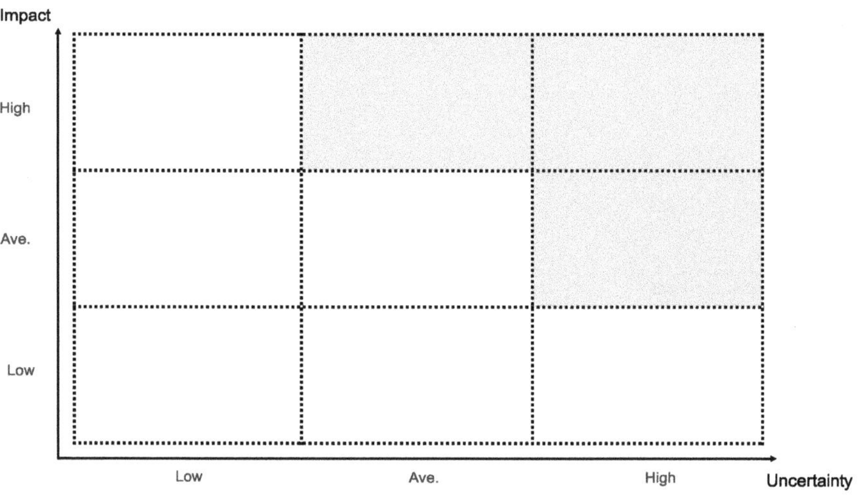
Impact
High
Ave.
Low
Low
Ave.
High
Uncertainty

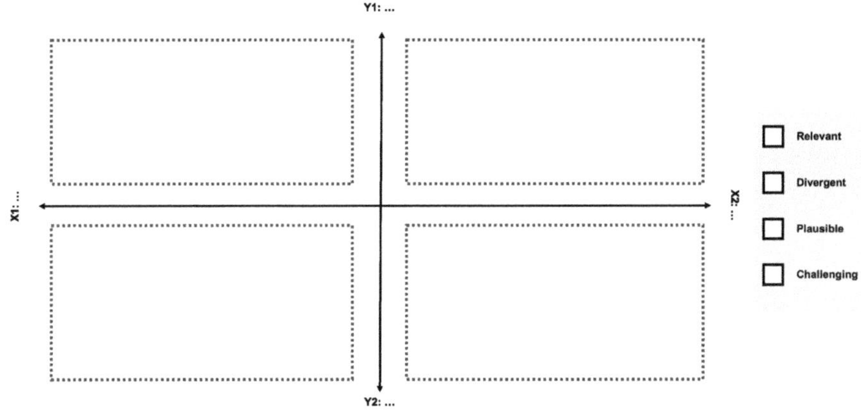

Y1: ...
Y2: ...
X1: ...
X2: ...
Relevant
Divergent
Plausible
Challenging

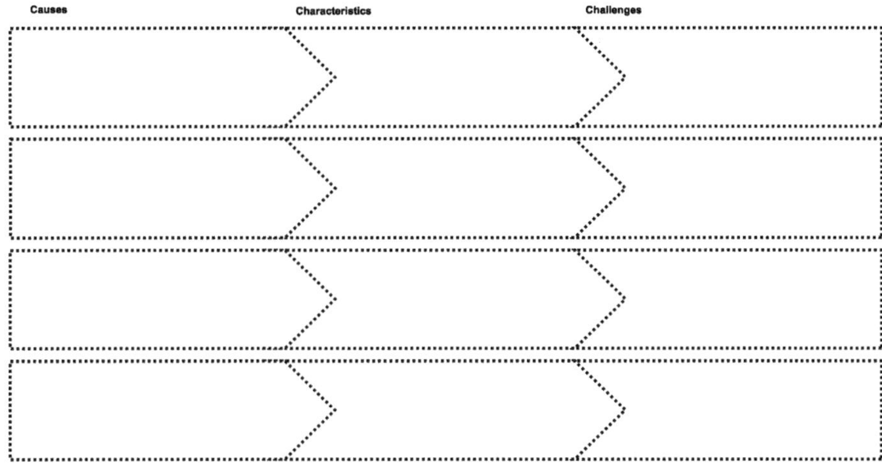

Causes
Characteristics
Challenges

Implications scenario ...

Options scenario...

💡 Option	Scenario 1:	Scenario 2:	Scenario 3:	Scenario 4:

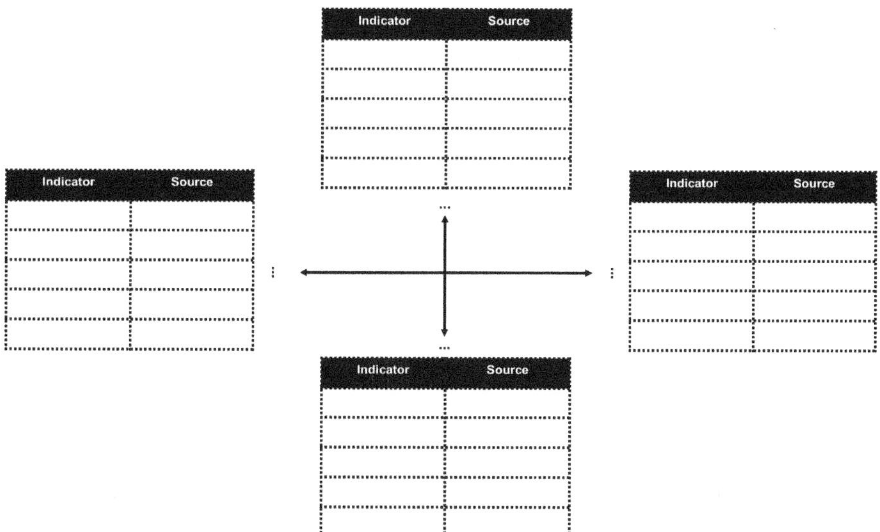

- Adams, D. (1979), *The Hitchhiker's Guide to the Galaxy*, London: Pan Books.
- Cohen, M.D. and P. Bacdayan (1994), "Organizational Routines Are Stored as Procedural Memory" in *Organizational Science*, 5, No. 4. The Institute of Management Sciences.
- Courtney, H. (2001), *20/20 Foresight. Crafting Strategy in an Uncertain World*, Boston: Harvard Business School Press.
- Courtney, H., J. Kirkland and P. Viguerie (1997), *Strategy Under Uncertainty*, in Harvard Business Review November-December 1997.
- Geus, A.P. de, (1988), *Planning as Learning*, in Harvard Business Review, March-April 1988.
- Godet, M. (1987), *Scenarios and Strategic Management*, London: Butterworths Scientific.
- Groot, T.L.C.M., and G.J. van Helden (2000), *Management control van non-profitorganisaties*, in Handboek Management Accounting.
- Heijden, K. van der (1998), "Scenario Planning: Scaffolding Disorganized Ideas about the Future" in *Forecasting with Judgment*, John Wiley & Sons Ltd.
- Heijden, K. van der (1997), *Strategy, and the Strategy Process* [presearch], Nyenrode University Press.
- Kelly, E. and S. Weber (2006), *A delicate balance between risk and reward*, in Financial Times, 8 September 2005.
- Lindgren, M. and H. Banhold (2003), *Scenarioplanning: the link between future and strategy*, New York: Palgrave MacMillan.

- Porter, M. (1985), *Competitive Advantage: Creating and Sustaining Superior Performance*, New York: Free Press
- Schnaars, S.P. (1986), "How to Develop Business Strategies from Multiple Scenarios", in *Handbook of Business Strategy*, Boston: Warran, Gosham and Lamont.
- Schoemaker, P.J.H. (1997), *Disciplined Imagination, From Scenarios to Strategic Options,* in International Studies of Management & Organization, Vol. 27, No. 2, Summer 1997, pp. 43-70.
- Schoemaker, P.J.H. (2002), *Profiting from Uncertainty: Strategies for Succeeding No Matter*
- Schwartz, P. (1991), *The Art of the Long View. Planning for the Future in an Uncertain World*, New York: Currency Doubleday

Michiel de Vries is a consultant, entrepreneur, and author. He is the founder of Jester Strategy. Global Business Network's Peter Schwartz taught him scenario planning. Michiel has previously authored other books in which scenario planning was featured. His book *Strategic Control* (Breunesse and De Vries, Kluwer 2011) deals with applying scenario planning to internal supervision on strategy. His book *City Strategy* (De Vries and Van Hanswijk Pennink, Eburon 2012) details how scenario planning can be of great value in strategy formulation for cities and regions. His book *Klaar voor de Toekomst* (De Vries, Nubiz 2021) presents a strategy approach for organizations that includes scenario planning. Michiel has been working with Jeroen Toet since 2009.

Jeroen Toet is senior consultant at Jester Strategy. He has become a scenario planning expert over the past fifteen years. In his capacity as a consultant he has worked on hundreds of scenario planning projects, ranging from compact 'pressure cooker' sessions to extensive multi-month, multi-stakeholder scenario projects in both private and public sectors across the globe. He is also guest lecturer at the Rotterdam School of Management on scenario planning. He publishes regularly about the impact of trends and uncertainties and is a frequent keynote speaker on those topics.